THE
ROYAL
GEOGRAPHICAL
SOCIETY
PUZZLE BOOK

THE
ROYAL
GEOGRAPHICAL
SOCIETY
PUZZLE BOOK

By

Royal Geographical Society (with IBG)

and

Nathan Joyce

Royal
Geographical
Society
Enterprises

Commercial activities
supporting the charity

Published by 535
The Plaza,
535 Kings Road,
Chelsea Harbour,
London, SW10 0SZ

twitter.com/535Books

Trade Paperback – 978-1-788702-96-6
Ebook – 978-1-788702-37-9

A CIP catalogue of this book is available from the British Library.

Designed by Envy Design Ltd
Printed and bound in Great Britain by Clays Ltd, Elcograf S.p.A

1 3 5 7 9 10 8 6 4 2

All images © Royal Geographical Society except Alamy © p.2, p.8, p.28, p.34,
p.82, p.134, p.140, p.146, p.150, p.178, p.196, p.200, p.203, p.224. Getty © p.38,
p.47, p.60, p.113, p.128, p.145, p.170, p.206, p.209, p.216, p.220. Colour Sections
– Shutterstock © flags from colour section 1 and 2, Getty © Ptolemy
and Ibn Battuta image.

Royal
Geographical
Society
Enterprises

Commercial activities
supporting the charity

MIX
Paper from
responsible sources
FSC® C018072
FSC
www.fsc.org

535 is an imprint of Bonnier Books UK
www.bonnierbooks.co.uk

'The difficult is what takes a little time;
the impossible is what takes a little longer.'

– FRIDTJOF NANSEN

CONTENTS

FOREWORD

From early accounts of Herodotus, the ancient Greek historian, who described the concealment of secret messages beneath wax on wooden tablets, to the flags and signals used by the 15th century Chinese admiral, Zheng He, codes and puzzles have always played an important part in both securing and protecting information for travellers, whilst also providing leisure-time distraction and a diversion for those undertaking fieldwork and expeditions.

During the British National Antarctic Expedition (1901–1904) initiated and led by the Society – more commonly known today as the *Discovery* expedition – Captain Robert Falcon Scott created the *South Polar Times*, an on-board magazine written by – and for – the expedition party to share their geographical knowledge on this first scientific expedition to the continent. Scott wanted to encourage and stimulate mental agility through puzzles in the form of a series of monthly acrostics, in which letters in the lines of a poem form words or phrases, for which points and even medals were awarded.

Sir Ernest Shackleton's *Endurance* Antarctic expedition of 1914–1917 had a well-stocked library. In addition to plays, novels and poetry, the books selected for the journey also included almanacs and encyclopaedias which provided much needed diversion and the best source for trivia and facts to fuel word games and quizzes. This communal activity became a common way to engage the brain during 'down time' on all later 'heroic age' expeditions in the Antarctic at the start of the 20th century.

At the world's highest altitudes, cryptic codes were often employed to minimise the leak of important news. The Society, providing science, survey, mapping and other technical expertise co-organised seven expeditions from the early 1920s with the Alpine Club London, under the auspices of the Mount Everest Committee. In 1924, following the tragic loss of George Mallory and Sandy Irvine on the mountain, a coded telegram was taken by runner to the Tibetan town of Phari Dzong. From there it was sent by telegram to London, reading, 'Mallory and Irvine Nove Remainder Alcedo', which translated as 'Mallory and Irvine killed in last engagement, arrived here, all in good order.' 'Nove' announced the deaths, whilst 'Alcedo' that the others were unhurt.

By contrast, during the 1953 attempt to reach the summit of Everest, on an expedition in which the Society provided the scientific and surveying expertise, whilst waiting for news of the hoped-for successful outcome of the attempt by Edmund Hillary and Tenzing Norgay, journalist James Morris tried to distract himself with completion of a part-finished crossword, but could think of nothing but the growing size of the 'tiny dots' as the men returned from their attempt. On achieving his scoop, Morris, employed by *The Times* of London, sent the message of the expedition's success to the newspaper in code, reading: 'Snow conditions bad stop advanced base abandoned May twenty-nine stop awaiting improvement stop all well.' This would have read as bad news to any interceptor of the telegram – but the paper's editors in London, who received it on the afternoon of 1st June 1953, were ecstatic, because decoded it read: 'Everest Climbed Hillary Tenzing May 29'.

Before exploring this Society puzzle book, why not try your hand at this original puzzle from the *South Polar Times* of April 1902. It is a double acrostic, where the initial and final letters of the one word answer to each question read downwards form the answer and the subject of the four line verse at the top (the answer is in the answer section):

From day to day the traveller bold
In polar regions, I am told
Thinks much of this; indeed it may
Be said to cheer him all the way.

1

Though found in myth, a word sometimes used,
A creature whose license was often abused.

2

Turkey may be the clue to invoke it

So now put that in your pipe and smoke it.

3

It o'ertops creation, yet still we may find

Some parts of this Southland are not far behind.

4

Perhaps your divinity hunts, if so

She may give you a clue to this word, you know.

5

Many are dark and some are damp too,

And one very famous example is blue.

6

Though in it the ploughman homeward may plod

There's one thing that's certain it never is odd.

Enjoy the book!

Professor Joe Smith

Director, Royal Geographical Society (with IBG)

September 2019

INTRODUCTION

For over 180 years, the Royal Geographical Society (with the Institute of British Geographers) has been advancing geographical knowledge about our world.

Today, we are the UK's learned Society and professional body for the subject, supporting geography and geographers around the world. With over 16,000 members, the Society promotes awareness and encourages debate around geographical subjects and provides a wide range of educational and public events and access to its 2-million strong collection of books, maps, artefacts, photographs and archive material linked to over 500 years of geographical discovery and engagement. Everyone can join.

We hope that you will enjoy exploring this puzzle book, which reflects on a range of historical and contemporary figures associated with the Society and its Collections and be inspired to find out a little more about what we do as a contemporary organisation supporting fieldwork and expeditions as well as a host of other activities at: www.rgs.org.

Happy puzzling!

The team at the Royal Geographical Society (with IBG)

THE
PUZZLES

MARCO POLO

FOLLOWING THE SILK ROAD
TO XANADU

In 1266 Niccolò and Maffeo Polo, Venetian jewel merchants, travelled to the court of Kublai Khan (1215–1294), the fifth Great Khan of the Mongol Empire. The Great Khan requested the brothers return to Europe as his envoys to the pope in Rome. The brothers returned to Venice in 1269 but set off for China again two years later, this time taking Niccolò's 17-year-old son, Marco Polo (1254–1324), with them. They followed an overland route, arriving in China in the summer of 1275, when Kublai Khan's court had moved to the Khan's lavish palace in Xanadu. Such was its legendary splendour that the word 'Xanadu' became a metaphor for opulence. Marco Polo became a great favourite of Kublai Khan and acted as his ambassador for nearly twenty years, travelling extensively around East Asia and collecting information on the people living in the various regions of the great Mongol empire.

Can you solve these Xanadu-themed quiz questions?

1. Xanadu was the name of the mansion owned by the eponymous character in which celebrated Hollywood film of 1941?

2. *Xanadu* was a romantic musical film, starring Olivia Newton-John, which was a legendary box office flop. It was so terrible that it inspired the creation of which mock booby prize awards to 'honour' the worst film of the year?

3. Madame Xanadu is the name of a fictional sorceress dreamed up by which iconic American comic book publishing company?

4. Xanadu is the name of a vast area of highly reflective ice on Titan, the largest of the 60-plus moons orbiting which planet?

5. Xanadu 2.0 is the nickname of a mansion on the edge of Lake Washington near Seattle valued at $178,348,725 in 2018. Which bespectacled American businessman is the owner?

BRAINTEASER: Xanadu features in the famous poem 'Kubla Khan', composed after an opium-induced dream in 1797 by which English poet?

'I HAVE ONLY TOLD YOU
HALF OF WHAT I SAW'

On his return to Venice in 1295 Marco Polo found Venice at war with the Republic of Genoa. Polo had travelled over 15,000 miles during a 24-year expedition of discovery, but he was captured during a naval battle and imprisoned in Genoa, spending several months dictating his remarkable adventures to fellow inmate Rustichello da Pisa. These stories became *The Travels of Marco Polo*, published around 1300. On his deathbed in 1323, in answer to claims that he had fabricated or embellished parts of his travels, he famously said: 'I have only told you half of what I saw.'

Marco Polo's travels included encounters with lands, creatures and objects, many of which Europeans had never heard of.

See if you can work out what he's describing from the passages in *The Travels of Marco Polo*:

1. Which creature is Marco Polo describing here ready for the King of Mien and Bangala to use in battle against the Great Khan in 1272?

   'So this king prepared a great force and munitions of war; and he had, let me tell you, 2,000 great _____, on each of which was set a tower of timber, well framed and strong, and carrying from twelve to sixteen well-armed fighting men.'

2. Which ferocious creature does Marco Polo describe here?

'The head is very big, and the eyes are bigger than a great loaf of bread. The mouth is large enough to swallow a man whole, and is garnished with great [pointed] teeth. And in short they are so fierce-looking and so hideously ugly, that every man and beast must stand in fear and trembling of them.'

3. What does he mistake a unicorn for here?

'There are wild elephants in the country, and numerous unicorns, which are very nearly as big... The head resembles that of a wild boar, and they carry it ever bent towards the ground. 'Tis a passing ugly beast to look upon, and is not in the least like that which our stories tell of as being caught in the lap of a virgin; in fact, 'tis altogether different from what we fancied.'

4. What does Marco Polo describe the Mongols using for small change?

'They have gold in rods, which they weigh, and they reckon its value by its weight in saggi, but they have no coined money. Their small change again is made in this way. They have _____ which they boil and set in a mould [flat below and round above]. Now, 80 moulds of this _____ are worth one saggio of fine gold. ... So this _____ serves them for small change.'

5. Marco Polo provides one of the earliest recorded accounts of which country?

'Cipangu is an island to the sunrising which is on the high sea 1,500 miles distant from the land of Mangi. It is an exceedingly great island. The people are… fair fashioned and beautiful. … The Lord that is the chief ruler of that island has a palace which is all covered with sheets of fine gold.'

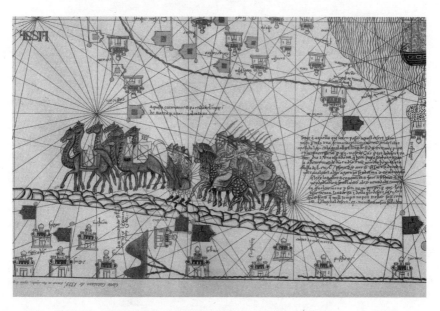

Marco Polo travelling with a camel caravan along the Silk Road. Detail from the 19th Century Santarem reproduction of the *Catalan Atlas* of 1375.

MYTH DEBUNKED! Polo familiarised Europeans with many Chinese contraptions, inventions and ideas including paper money but he did not introduce pasta to Italy. It had already existed in Europe for centuries.

ZHENG HE

INTREPID MING DYNASTY
EXPLORER

Zheng He (1371–1435) was a Chinese explorer who made several pioneering voyages to South Asia, Western Asia and the Middle East between 1405 and 1433. The Chinese Emperor Yongle initiated an ambitious maritime programme after China's overland trade routes had been devastated by the Mongol ruler Timur. Zheng was chosen to command the 'treasure fleet', so called because of the vast wealth carried on board to project Chinese influence far and wide. At ports along the way, gifts were offered and Chinese authority was asserted, sometimes by force. The fleet initially comprised 300 ships and 28,000 men, the like of which would not be seen again until the Second World War.

Although the expeditions did not lead to a trading empire being established, they increased China's political sway over maritime Asia, paving the way for extensive Chinese emigration and eventual colonisation.

Can you identify the places Zheng He visited during his seven expeditions from the cryptic clues below and add them to the map opposite?

1. That's President Bartlet to you – Russian affirmative

2. Female parent – edible cobbler

3. Informal word for a cat – basic arithmetic operation – the middle and end of a sneeze

4. Humanitarian assistance – canine home

5. Bad entries into water

6. Strike noisily – rooster

7. Large cove – first syllable of the title of a famous Christmas song originally called 'One Horse Open Sleigh'

8. Raincoat – female whale

9. Flatbread – ruler

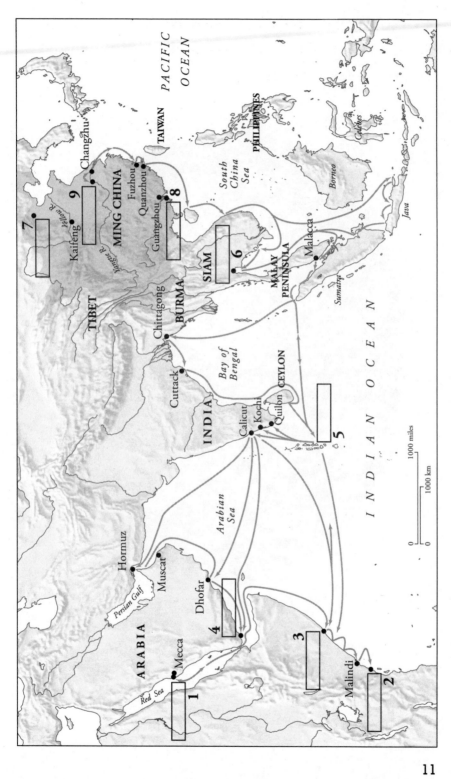

PACIFIC OCEAN

TAIWAN

Changzhu

MING CHINA

Kaifeng

Yellow R.

Fuzhou
Quanzhou

9

7

Guangzhou

8

TIBET

BURMA

SIAM

6

Chittagong

South China Sea

PHILIPPINES

Borneo

Celebes

Malacca

MALAY PENINSULA

Sumatra

Java

Bay of Bengal

Cuttack

INDIA

CEYLON

Calicut
Kochi
Quilon

5

Hormuz

Persian Gulf

Muscat

Arabian Sea

Dhofar

4

INDIAN OCEAN

ARABIA

Mecca

Red Sea

1

3

Malindi

2

1000 miles

1000 km

11

12

FERDINAND MAGELLAN

THE FIRST CIRCUMNAVIGATION (NEARLY) OF THE WORLD

Ferdinand Magellan (1480–1521) was a Portuguese explorer and navigator who formally led an expedition to circumnavigate the world in 1519, a feat completed by Spanish explorer Juan Sebastián Elcano following the death of Magellan in the Philippines in 1521.

Can you fill in the missing blanks in the story of Magellan's voyage that begins on the next page?

starvation	baptised
masts	gold
38	Spice Islands
pearls	Sea of the South
mirror	Gulf of Cadiz
Cape Verde	anchor line
Equator	quicksilver
mutinied	seven

set alight	marooned
scurvy	Cape of Good Hope
banquet	spectacles
Canary Islands	deserted
1,500	Tierra del Fuego
Cape Horn	18
Brazil	executed
cinnamon	Magellan Straits
50	ox hides
Philippines	99

In 1517, after a quarrel with King Manuel I of Portugal, Ferdinand Magellan (*c*.1480–1521) renounced his Portuguese nationality to lead a Spanish-funded voyage to the Moluccas – also known as the _____. The successful completion of the mission would mean control of trade during a period of fierce rivalry between Spain and Portugal, which historian Laurence Bergreen describes as 'the Renaissance equivalent of winning the space race'. Magellan never intended to circumnavigate the globe and, indeed, he didn't.

King Charles I of Spain supplied a fleet of five ships, the flagship *Trinidad*, under Magellan's command, the *San Antonio*, the *Concepción*, the *Santiago* and the *Victoria* with approximately 265 men. There were around 37 Portuguese, including Magellan's brother-in-law, Duarte Barbosa.

On 10th August 1519, the fleet set sail from the Guadalquivir river in Seville, Spain, making for the _____ and into the Atlantic Ocean. They reached the _____ on 26th September to replenish supplies before heading south along the west coast of Africa. They crossed the _____ in October 1519 and continued southwest, reaching the coast of _____ in December.

To ride out the Southern Hemisphere winter, Magellan established the settlement Puerto San Julián in Patagonia on 31st March 1520. The following day, tragedy struck. Magellan's three Spanish captains _____. Magellan responded swiftly and decisively. He sent a raiding party to retake the *Victoria*, killing the disloyal captain Luis de Mendoza. Magellan also deployed a small force to secretly sever the _____ of the *Concepción*, commanded by Gaspar de Quesada. The ship drifted towards Magellan's flagship. Faced with the better-armed *Trinidad*, Captain de Quesada surrendered, as did Juan de Cartagena, the captain of the *San Antonio*.

De Cartagena was _____ on the Patagonian coast by means of punishment. While some of the mutineers were _____, most were spared, as Magellan would not have been able to continue on without them. One of the spared men was the sailing master of the *Concepción*, Juan Sebastián Elcano, who would go on to play a pivotal role in the subsequent journey. Meanwhile, Magellan placed his dependable brother-in-law Duarte Barbosa in command of the *Victoria*.

Travelling south along the east coast of South America, Magellan searched for the entrance to the navigable sea route through southern Chile rather than attempt the even more perilous journey around _____. On 21st October 1520, after reaching Cape Virgenes, Magellan declared that they had found the passageway. He observed numerous fires on the shores of the coast and aptly named the area _____.

From here, they commenced a treacherous voyage through the passageway, which took _____ days. Magellan called it *Estrecho de Todos los Santos* (All Saints' Channel) but this was later renamed the _____ in his honour.

San Antonio deserted on 20th November and returned home to Spain, while the *Santiago* was shipwrecked during a scouting expedition. All of the crew survived in a heroic rescue mission. On 28th November, the remaining three ships cleared the straits, entering what was then known as the _____, which Magellan renamed the Mar Pacifico (Pacific Ocean) on account of its tranquil waters.

From here, Magellan began the arduous journey across the ocean. Many of the crew succumbed to _____ and thirst. In desperation, they turned to the worm-riddled biscuit crumbs that reeked of rat urine, along with sawdust and the _____ on the _____.

The remaining ships crossed the Equator on 13th February. They sighted two islands, but both were_____, earning them the name the 'Unfortunate Isles'. Finally, on 6 March they made landfall at Guam in the Mariana Islands, obtaining fresh food and water for the first time in _____ days. While the ship was anchored, many of the island's inhabitants stole whatever they could from the ships, including the small boat fastened to the *Trinidad*. Magellan was forced to deploy troops to retake the boat, killing natives and burning houses in the process. He later named the islands the 'Ladrones' or 'Thieving Islands'.

On 16th March, Magellan sighted the first of the _____. They relied on Magellan's indentured servant Enrique, whom he bought after the Portuguese conquest of Malacca in 1511, to communicate with the native peoples. On 7th April, they arrived at Cebu and made an alliance with the Rajah and his queen, who consented to be _____. The Rajah convinced Magellan to kill Lapu-Lapu, an enemy of his who ruled the island of Mactan.

Magellan arrived at Mactan on 27th April 1521 with a force of around _____ but was faced with an army numbering approximately _____. Approaching the shore in knee-high water, Magellan was spotted, targeted by large numbers of assailants and killed in the ensuing skirmish. Antonio Pigafetta, the Venetian scholar on board the *Trinidad*, who recorded the details of their epic journey, lamented Magellan's loss thus: they 'killed our _____, our light, our comfort, and our true guide'.

Barbosa and João de Serrão, the former captain of the *Santiago*, were chosen as leaders. Meanwhile, Magellan's last will and testament provided for Enrique's freedom, but this was refused and he was threatened by Barbosa and Serrão. The furious Enrique conspired with the Rajah of Cebu, who arranged a _____ on 1st May and massacred Barbosa, Serrão and 24 others, securing Enrique his freedom.

With too few sailors to man the three remaining ships, the *Concepción* was _____ and crew members transferred to the *Trinidad* and *Victoria*. They landed at Borneo, with _____ men going ashore bearing gifts for the ruler, Rajah Siripada. The Europeans traded their merchandise of bronze, glass, cinnabar, wool cloth and linens although iron and _____ were the most highly prized. Pigafetta describes that the inhabitants drank _____ to cure ailments. In the Rajah's palace were two _____ as large as hen's eggs.

They successfully reached the Spice Islands on 6th November 1521 and traded with the Sultan of Tidore for cloves and _____. Laden with goods that were worth more than their weight in _____, the two ships made for Spain. By 6th May 1522, the *Victoria* rounded the _____. Their supplies had dwindled to grains of rice, and 20 men died of _____.

The *Trinidad* was captured by Portuguese forces and later shipwrecked, but the *Victoria*, captained by Elcano, made it to _____ and onwards to Seville, completing the first circumnavigation of the earth. Only _____ men had survived the epic voyage.

> **FASCINATING FACT:** While Elcano is regarded as the first person to circumnavigate the globe, the honour may arguably belong to Magellan's servant Enrique of Malacca. After escaping in May 1521 and returning to his homeland, where he had been captured ten years previously, he effectively circumnavigated the globe, albeit indirectly and against his will.

HERNÁN CORTÉS

RUTHLESS CONQUEROR OF
THE AZTEC EMPIRE

Hernán Cortés (1485–1547) was a Spanish explorer and conquistador who famously brought about the fall of the Aztec Empire. Born into a noble family with grand titles but few resources, Cortés had to make his name by leaving Spain for the New World. He sailed to Hispaniola in 1504, aged just 18, before helping to conquer the neighbouring island of Cuba in 1506 under Diego Velázquez who became the first governor of the new Spanish colony. It wasn't until 1518 that Velázquez gave Cortés command of an expedition to conquer the interior of Mexico. Cortés was determined to conquer the Aztecs and secured alliances with at least two indigenous peoples who had been subjugated by them. He began the march on the capital Tenochtitlán in August 1519 and took Moctezuma II, the Aztec emperor, hostage in November 1519. He finally defeated the Aztecs in August 1521, securing the land of Mexico and its vast wealth for the Spanish crown.

His legacy is controversial, not least for the great cruelty he inflicted on the indigenous population. At the end of the conquest, 200,000 Aztecs had been slain or perished due to their lack of immunity to diseases introduced from Europe.

FASCINATING FACT: Cortés died of pleurisy in December 1547. For over 400 years, his remains were transported to various locations in Spain and Mexico. In all, he was buried and exhumed nine times. Amid the rising tide of nationalism and Mexico's declaration of independence in 1821, conservative politician Lucas Alamán saved Cortés' body from desecration, secretly burying it and moving it again 13 years later. He revealed the body's location in a letter to the Spanish Embassy but this remained sealed in a vault for 123 years. Finally, in 1946, the true resting place was revealed and he was reburied in the Church of the Immaculate Conception and Jesus the Nazarene in Mexico City.

See if you can conquer this multiple choice quiz on this conquistador

1. Cortés was the_____ of fellow conquistador Francisco Pizarro, who conquered the Inca Empire.

   A: Brother-in-law   B: Second cousin once removed
   C: Stepfather

2. Before travelling to Hispaniola, Cortés initially trained to be a _____.

   A: Lawyer   B: Accountant   C: Tax collector

3. At the time of its conquest, Tenochtitlán was one of the largest cities in the world with a population estimated to have been between _____ and _____.

A: 10,000 and 20,000   B: 100,000 and 200,000
C: 200,000 and 300,000

4. To eliminate any ideas of retreat, Cortés _____ to commit his forces to survival by conquest.

A: Scuttled his ships   B: Deliberately destroyed their own supplies   C: Executed his sailors

5. The Aztecs sacrificed their Spanish captors by removing their _____ to offer them to their idols.

A: Heads   B: Livers   C: Hearts

6. An epidemic of _____ broke out in Tenochtitlán in late October 1520 decimating the population.

A: Bubonic plague   B: Smallpox   C: Cholera

7. In June 1520, while fleeing Tenochtitlán, some Spaniards drowned in the surrounding marshes weighed down by the _____ they had carried off.

A: Gold   B: Silver   C: Platinum

8. Moctezuma drank copious quantities of _____ served in gold cups.

   A: Coffee   B: Cocoa   C: Wine

9. Cortés ordered the torture of Moctezuma's successor Cuauhtemoc, _____ _____ _____ to try and force the emperor to reveal hidden gold stashes.

   A: Cutting off his ears   B: Branding his chest
   C: Burning his feet

10. The Spanish built _____ on the ruins of Tenochtitlán.

    A: Mexico City   B: Oaxaca   C: Acapulco

THE ROAD TO TENOCHTITLÁN

Cortés landed at a place he would name Veracruz in the land of the Totonacs in July 1519 and attempted to arrange a meeting with the *tlatoani* (ruler) of the Aztec Empire, Moctezuma II. He refused but Cortés managed to negotiate with the Totonacs, who appealed to him 'to protect them against the mighty Lord [Moctezuma], who used violent and tyrannical measures to keep them in subjection, and took from them their sons to be slain and offered as sacrifices to his idols'. Cortés now had an ally who knew the way to Tenochtitlán. In August 1519, Cortés marched there with just over 500 soldiers, 16 horses, 14 cannons, and thousands of indigenous carriers and warriors.

Can you plot Cortés' route to the city of Tenochtitlán on the map on the next page by solving the anagrams and finding the names of the places he visited along the way? Note that he visited one place twice

1. MAZE OPAL
2. CIRCULARIZED LARVA VEAL
3. MAZE OPAL
4. A PAL AX
5. AXAU INCH
6. CLAIM TAXI ANT TAX
7. CALL A TAX
8. OUCH ALL
9. MACE ACE MA
10. QUICMIX
11. ZIT ALA PAPA
12. CLOTHE TIN ANT

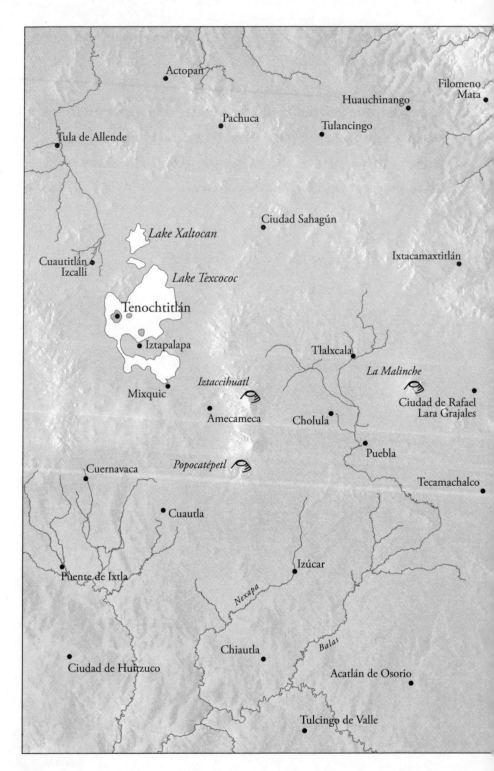

Actopan

Filomeno
Mata

Huauchinango

Pachuca

Tulancingo

Tula de Allende

Ciudad Sahagún

Lake Xaltocan

Ixtacamaxtitlán

Cuautitlán
Izcalli

Lake Texcococ

Tenochtitlán

Iztapalapa

Tlalxcala

La Malinche

Iztaccihuatl

Ciudad de Rafael
Lara Grajales

Mixquic

Amecameca

Cholula

Puebla

Popocatépetl

Cuernavaca

Tecamachalco

Cuautla

Izúcar

Puente de Ixtla

Nexapa

Balas

Chiautla

Ciudad de Huitzuco

Acatlán de Osorio

Tulcingo de Valle

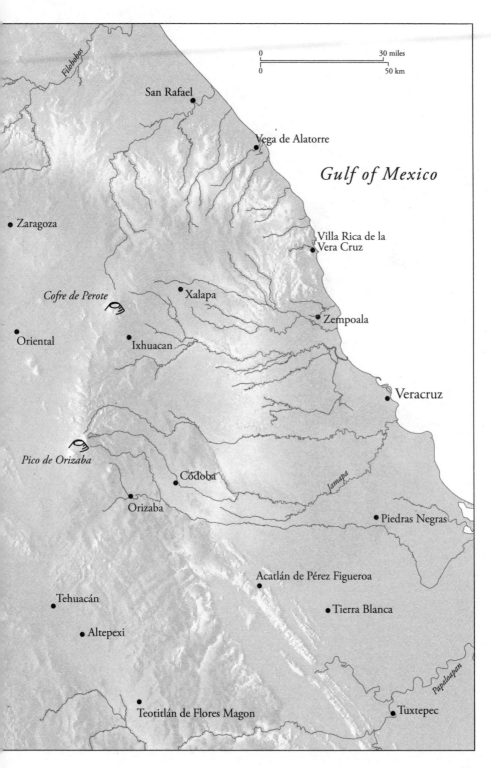

San Rafael

Vega de Alatorre

Gulf of Mexico

Zaragoza

Villa Rica de la
Vera Cruz

Cofre de Perote

Xalapa

Zempoala

Oriental

Ixhuacan

Veracruz

Pico de Orizaba

Códoba

Jamapa

Orizaba

Piedras Negras

Acatlán de Pérez Figueroa

Tehuacán

Tierra Blanca

Altepexi

Papaloapan

Teotitlán de Flores Magon

Tuxtepec

Filobobos

0   30 miles

0   50 km

ESTEVANICO

THE TRAVELS OF AN
EXTRAORDINARY SLAVE

Estevanico (*c.*1500–1539) was born in Morocco and enslaved as a youth by the conquering Portuguese. After being sold to the Spanish nobleman Andrés Dorantes de Carranza, Estevanico was taken on the Narváez expedition of 1527 – a journey of exploration led by Pánfilo de Narváez that sought to found colonial settlements in Florida. Of the 300 men who embarked upon the expedition, only Estevanico and three Spaniards (including Dorantes) survived, only to be coerced into becoming medicine men by the indigenous population. After their methods proved effective, they were treated with great respect, attracting crowds numbering many thousands, and eventually made their way to Mexico City.

Fascinated by their tale, the Viceroy of New Spain (Mexico) asked the three Spaniards to lead an expedition northwards, but they refused. Estevanico was bought by or sold to the Viceroy and used as a guide for a 1539 expedition to find the fabled Seven Cities of Gold. Travelling into northwest New Mexico, he was greeted with distrust by the local Zuni people and was murdered.

Estevanico travelled along the coast of the USA and into several modern USA states. Can you guess the states from the trivia clues provided?

You can try either of the two quizzes below: the first is general knowledge, while the second will test your music knowledge. Both have the same answers!

GENERAL KNOWLEDGE TRIVIA
1. Grand Canyon State
2. 'Dubya'
3. Counting aloud
4. Forrest Gump's home state
5. Launch pad of the Space Shuttle
6. Sun King
7. Alien landing site, 1947?

MUSIC TRIVIA
The following song lyrics reference either the name of a state or the name of a major city in the state. Name the state!

1. 'Standing on a corner in Winslow,_____'

2. 'All my ex's live in_____'

3. 'Getting born in the state of _____, Papa was a copper, and her mama was a hippy'

4. 'In _____ they love the Gov'nor'

5. 'All night on the beach till the break of dawn, Welcome to _____'

6. 'There is a house in _____, they call the rising sun'

7. 'Hot dog, jumping frog,_____'

FASCINATING FACT: Spanish voices of dissent against the brutality of the conquistadors began to emerge in the early 16th century. Bartolomé de las Casas, a Dominican priest who emigrated to Hispaniola in 1502, wrote of his shock at the brutality of the *encomienda* system of indigenous slavery and the subsequent mass slaughter of Cuban tribes by Spanish soldiers. His eyewitness accounts would contribute to some of the earliest forms of human rights law.

FRANCIS DRAKE

FIRST ENGLISHMAN TO CIRCUMNAVIGATE THE GLOBE

Francis Drake (1540–1596) was an English privateer, naval officer and explorer. After making several successful raids on Spanish shipping in the 1570s and capturing a frigate with over £20,000 of booty, in 1577 he embarked on a voyage along the coast of the Americas that would eventually take him round the world. He returned a hero in 1580 with such a vast quantity of treasure and spices that he helped pay off England's national debt.

> **TRIVIA:** When the *Elizabeth*, captained by John Wynter, separated from the *Golden Hind* in 1578 during a storm near Cape Horn, Wynter sent a boat ashore to seek medicinal herbs, probably on account of a scurvy outbreak. They discovered trees bearing white flowers and made an infusion from the bark, which worked as a cure. The tree was later given the scientific name *Drimys winteri* in the captain's honour.

AWARD OF ARMS

Drake came from from humble origins, the eldest of 12 sons born to a Protestant farmer and his wife in Tavistock, Devon. In recognition of his remarkable exploits, he was knighted on 4th April 1581 aboard his ship the *Golden Hind*. Drake subsequently claimed kinship with the noble Drake family from Musbury, Devon but the head of the family, Bernard Drake, angrily refused any connection with Sir Francis. Such was the nature of the quarrel that the queen got involved, siding with her favourite and awarding him a new coat of arms.

Can you work out the English translations of the two Latin mottoes from the anagrams below?

LIVENED WHIP HIT
(Motto on left)

FORTHRIGHTNESS
HALTING
SMUG MALTS
(Motto under globe)

Drake's Crest.

Can you add the correct numbers to go with the labels on the map below to pinpoint where the following events happened?

1. Captures Portuguese merchant ship near Cape Verde Islands and adds captain Nuno da Silva, a skilled navigator of South America, to his crew

2. Abandons quest to find the western entrance of the Northwest Passage

3. The *Marigold* sinks in the Strait of Magellan

4. Executes former friend Thomas Doughty for treason at the port where Magellan faced a mutiny

5. Captures Spanish treasure galleon *Cacafuego*, laden with gold, silver and gems worth approximately £500 million today

6. Lands at the Spice Islands and trades for six tons of cloves at a 'very cheap [sic] rate'

7. Rounds a cape he describes as 'the fairest we saw in the whole circumference of the earth'

> **FASCINATING FACT:** According to *Forbes* magazine, Drake was the second highest-earning pirate in history, with an accumulated wealth of $140 million (at 2008 prices). Only Samuel 'Black Sam' Bellamy ($146 million) claimed more on the high seas.

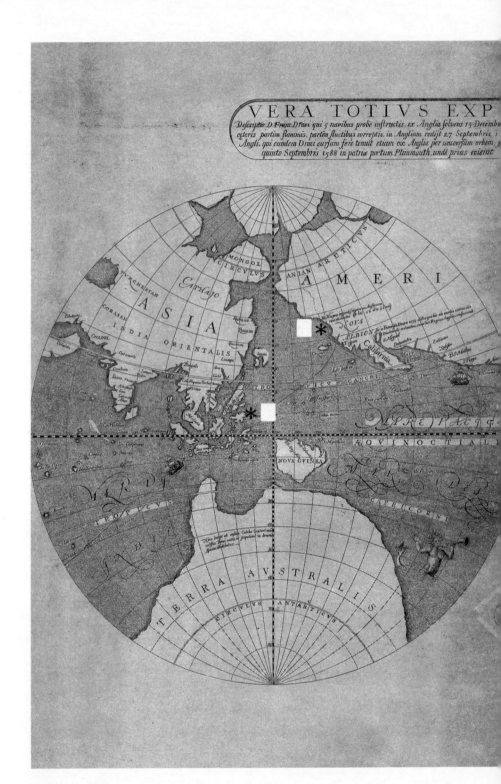

VERA TOTIVS EXP

Descriptio D. Franc. Draci qui 5. navibus probe instructis, ex Anglia solvens 13 Decembr ceteris partim flammis, partim fluctibus correptis, in Angliam redijt 27 Septembris i Angli, qui eundem Draci cursum fere tenuit etiam ex Anglia per universum orbem; quinto Septembris 1588 in patriæ portum Plinmouth, unde prius exierat

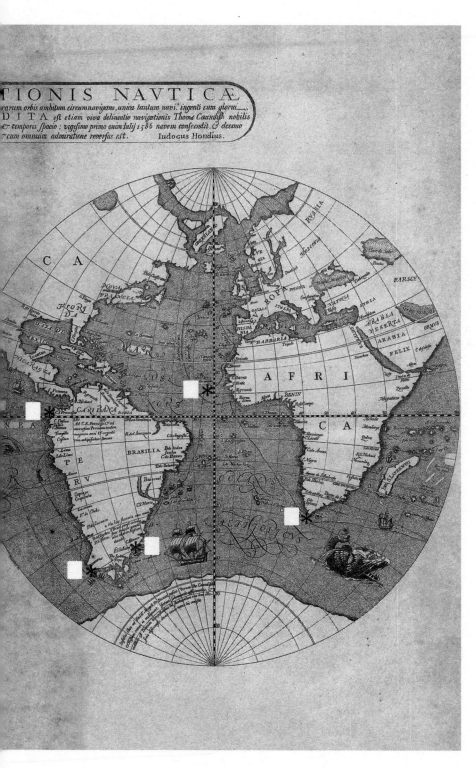

ABEL TASMAN

SEEKING THE GREAT
SOUTH LAND

Abel Tasman (1603–1659) was a Dutch navigator and explorer who, under the employ of the Dutch East India Company, embarked on two voyages to explore hitherto unknown parts of the southeastern Pacific. Anthony van Diemen, governor-general of the Dutch East Indies, entrusted Tasman with this crucial mission, which included finding the mythical 'Southern Continent'.

1. What name did Abel Tasman give to the island group that we now know as New Zealand? (Tip: it is the name of one of the islands south of Manhattan in New York)

   A: Liberty   B: Staten   C: Ellis

2. The image on page 40 shows the first European impression of which people?

   A: Maori   B: Papuans   C: Micronesians

3. On the morning after the first encounter with the indigenous people of New Zealand, a skirmish broke out which led to the deaths of several Europeans. What name did Tasman give to the bay where it happened?

A: Cutthroat Bay   B: Slaughterhouse Bay
C: Murderers' Bay

4. Tasman ordered two pigs for dinner and an extra ration of arrack (rice wine) to celebrate what occasion?

A: Christmas Day 1642   B: New Year's Day 1642
C: All Saints' Day 1642

5. 'We should have greatly liked to have come to anchor near one of these islands but could find no roadstead

on account of the numberless shoals and reefs that run out to sea from all these islands.'

Which Pacific archipelago comprising approximately 330 islands is Tasman describing?

A: Fiji   B: Tonga   C: Samoa

6. What endeavour did Tasman succeed in without realising it?

   A: Sailing closer to the Antarctic than any other European
   B: Circumnavigating Australia
   C: Circumnavigating New Zealand

7. Describing his first communication with the people of Tonga, what does Tasman trade for coconuts? '... a great number of prows came alongside, some of them with 5 or 6, others with 10 or 12 coconuts, all of which we bartered against _____?'

   A: Old corks   B: Old nails   C: Old rope

8. Pieter Jacobsz, the ship's carpenter, volunteered to swim to the shore of the newly named Van Diemen's Land to do what?

   A: Plant the Dutch flag
   B: Begin constructing the first building
   C: Fetch wood to fix a hole in the side of the ship

ABEL TASMAN – SOME MEN ARE ISLANDS

The following eight islands or archipelagos have all been
named after European explorers, navigators or naval officers
who either first 'discovered' them, visited or sighted them.
Some are countries in their own right, while others are
territories belonging to countries. **Can you guess them from
the clues?**

1. Previously known as the 'Isle of the Devils' and situated
   in an area associated with shipwrecks

2. Originally named Hervey Island by a famous English
   explorer hailing from North Yorkshire

3. Northernmost of the Canary Islands and the fourth
   largest after Tenerife, Fuerteventura and Gran Canaria

4. Populated mostly by descendants of the HMS *Bounty* mutineers

5. The most remote inhabited archipelago in the world, part of the British Overseas Territory of Saint Helena and Ascension, and named after a Portuguese explorer

6. The largest island in Canada, known for its population of polar bears

7. Named after a Dutch sea captain, this island forms part of the Shark Bay World Heritage Area off the west coast of Australia

8. Part of the island group Micronesia, this USA-associated state was used for nuclear testing between 1946 and 1958

RENÉ-ROBERT CAVELIER SIEUR DE LA SALLE

CLAIMING 'LA LOUISIANE' FOR FRANCE

Born in Normandy, France to a wealthy family, René-Robert Cavelier Sieur de la Salle (1643–1687) travelled to Montreal in 1666 and began his career as a pioneer farmer.

He returned to France in 1677 to seek King Louis XIV's permission to explore the 'western parts of New France' and to seek a monopoly in the buffalo hide trade. He canoed down the Illinois river and canoed down the Mississippi river, reaching the Mississippi delta on 6th April 1682. Reaching the Gulf of Mexico on 9th April, he claimed the river, its numerous tributaries and the surrounding lands for Louis XIV, naming it 'La Louisiane' in his honour.

In 1684, La Salle departed France once more and returned to the Gulf of Mexico to establish a French colony. The journey was plagued by navigational errors, desertions, sickness, and attacks by the indigenous population and by Spanish pirates.

Despite his courage and ambition, the ill-tempered and arrogant La Salle, who was famously disdainful to his subordinates, was shot dead by his own men on 19th March 1687.

> **FASCINATING FACT:** La Salle was poisoned twice by his own men but recovered both times. The first time he was served a salad containing leaves of hemlock. The second time, poison was administered to a pot in which his food was cooked, but he was saved by an antidote he had been given before he left France.

Can you work out which rivers in the USA are being referenced in the quotation below?

1. Which river did La Salle describe as 'the most tremendous river upon this globe . . . rushing down with a sort of maniacal fury, from its sources among the Rocky Mountains . . . to its entrance into the Gulf of Mexico.'

2. Which river, which La Salle claimed for France on 9th April 1682 at the junction of its delta near the Gulf of Mexico, was named the Colbert river after La Salle's patron and French finance minister Jean-Baptiste Colbert?

3. On which river did La Salle's servant perish after being seized by an alligator? Clue: It begins in the Rockies and carves its way down into the Gulf of California.

4. Which river forms part of the present-day border between Mexico and the USA, and formed the western boundary of the territory claimed by La Salle for France?

5. 'In the autumn of 1677 he left the fort in charge of his lieutenant, descended the _____ to Quebec, and sailed for France.' Which river, connecting the Great Lakes to the Atlantic Ocean, is being described here?

René-Robert Cavelier Sieur de la Salle stands at the mouth of the Mississippi river.

WILLIAM DAMPIER

'A MAN OF EXQUISITE MIND'

William Dampier (1651–1715) was an English buccaneer, explorer and naturalist, famous for visiting and charting 'New Holland' (the name given by Dutch explorers to present-day Australia). After joining the Royal Navy in 1673 and fighting in the Franco-Dutch War, he suffered a long illness and returned to England to recuperate. Dampier became a buccaneer in 1679, raiding Spanish shipping in the Caribbean, Pacific and East Indies. He finally returned to England in 1691, having circumnavigated the globe. He wrote the successful book *A New Voyage Round the World* (1697), which the Royal Navy were so impressed by that they granted Dampier command of the warship HMS *Roebuck* to undertake his proposed expedition to the east coast of New Holland. This was the Royal Navy's first mission dedicated to science and exploration.

See if you can identify places on the route Dampier took on board the HMS *Roebuck* by solving the following clues:

1. Archipelago that gave its name to a songbird connected to the coal mining industry

2. Green island nation

3. Spanish for 'Saviour'

4. The legendary home of the *Flying Dutchman*

5. Island destination of Captain William Bligh after the mutiny on HMS *Bounty*

6. Anagram: Wage ennui

7. Set to become the biggest city in the world with a population of 35.6 million by 2030

8. Napoleon Bonaparte's place of death

9. British Overseas Territory named after the departure of Christ from earth

---

BRAINTEASER: Which popular cooking apparatus evolved from a description Dampier gave of a sleeping platform above the ground used to minimise the risk of snakebite?

DAMPIER AND THE DICTIONARY

During the course of Dampier's circumnavigations and seven published works, he introduced approximately 1,000 new words to the English dictionary. **Can you name the items he is describing?**

1. 'They are seldom fit to eat till they have gathered two or three days; then they become soft, and the skin or rind will peel off.'

   (CLUE: stoned fruit)

2. ''Tis as big as a small Pear, somewhat long shaped, of a reddish colour, the rind pretty thick and rough, the inside white, inclosing a large black kernel, in shape like a Bean.'

   (CLUE: stoned fruit)

3. 'And tho; it be difficult for strangers to use them, being unaccustom'd to them, yet a little use will overcome that difficulty. They are as ordinarily placed at the Table here, as Knives, Forks, and Spoons are in *England*'

4. 'A Fruit as big as a Pippin, pretty long, and bigger near the Stemb than at the other end. The Seed of this Fruit grows at the end of it; 'tis of an Olive Colour shaped like a Bean'

   (CLUE: nut)

BRAINTEASER: Which famous 18th-century novel, inspired by Dampier's tales, was first published under the title *Travels into Several Remote Nations of the World*?

WILLIAM DAMPIER'S THIRD CIRCUMNAVIGATION 1708–1711

Sailing master William Dampier has received some extraordinary information from a Spanish captive. It transpires that the Scottish privateer Alexander Selkirk had been marooned four years ago by his captain on the uninhabited Más a Tierra island in the South Pacific Ocean. Until now, Selkirk had been presumed dead. Dampier intercepted a bottle that washed ashore containing the following message. Can you decipher it to reveal his coordinates in latitude and longitude (in degrees, minutes and seconds for both)?

Marooned! Please send help. Seek and ye shall find.
Alexander Selkirk

☐	☐	☐	☐	☐	☐

South   *West*

1. The number of bones in a human spine

2. The sum of the squares of the first three primes

3. C-L-XX-I

4. A complete set of Tarot cards

5. A golden wedding anniversary

6. The shortest month

BRAINTEASER: Which literary hero was Más a Tierra island renamed in honour of?

JAMES COOK

THE MAN WHO SAILED
'AS FAR AS I THINK IT POSSIBLE
FOR MAN TO GO'

James Cook (1728–1779) began his working life as a shop assistant in the fishing village of Staithes in Yorkshire before joining the merchant navy in his teens and the Royal Navy aged 27. Showing an aptitude for navigation and cartography, he was given the command of HMS *Grenville* in 1763, and tasked with surveying the coast of Newfoundland.

In 1768, he was appointed to lead a scientific mission to Tahiti to establish an observatory and measure the transit of Venus across the Sun. Joining the young lieutenant were the botanists Joseph Banks, Daniel Solander and Herman Spöring.

Returning to England in 1771, he was commissioned to undertake a second mission, to seek the great 'Southern Continent', known as *Terra Australis Incognita*. On his third voyage, he sought the elusive Northwest Passage in the Arctic, coming within 50 miles of the western entrance, but was repelled by terrible weather and ice floes. He was killed in the Sandwich Islands (Hawaii) when attempting to bring the King of Hawaii on board his ship. Among his many achievements, Cook was the first European to make contact with the east coast of Australia and the first to circumnavigate New Zealand.

What creatures is Cook describing here in questions 1–4?

1. 'As I was walking this morning at a little distance from the ship, I saw, myself, one of the animals which had been so often described: it was of a light mouse colour, and in size and shape very much resembling a greyhound; it had a long tail also, which it carried like a greyhound; and I should have taken it for a wild dog, if, instead of running, it had not leapt like a hare or deer...'

2. 'They lay in herds of many hundred upon the ice, huddling one over the other like swine, and roar or bray very loud, so that in the night or foggy weather they gave us notice of the ice long before we could see it.'

3. '...what the French call Nuance, and seem to be a middle species between bird and fish... and their wings themselves, which they use only in diving, and not to accelerate their motion even upon the surface of the water, may, perhaps with equal propriety, be called fins.'

4. 'He had observed that the large _____, of which there is great plenty in the bay, followed the flowing tide into very shallow water; he therefore took the opportunity of flood, and struck several in not more than two or three feet water: one of them weighed no less than two hundred and forty pounds after his entrails were taken out.'

5. What famous sight is Cook describing?
   'We could hardly conceive how these islanders, wholly unacquainted with any mechanical power, could raise such stupendous figures, and afterwards place the large cylindric stones before mentioned upon their heads.'

6. Which Pacific archipelago is Cook describing?
   'It was at first intended to perform this great, and now a principal business of our voyage, either at the Marquesas, or else at one of those islands which Tasman had called Amsterdam, Rotterdam, and Middleburg, now better known under the name of the Friendly Islands.'

7. What does 'antiscorbutick' [sic] mean?
   'As I intend to sail in the morning some hands were employ'd picking of Sellery to take to sea with us, this is found here (New Zealand) in great plenty and I have caused it to be boiled with Portable Soup and Oatmeal every morning for the Peoples breakfast, and this I design to continue as long as it will last or any is to be

got, because I look upon it to be very wholesome and a great Antiscorbutick.'

8. What famous Australian coastal area, where Cook first made landfall, is being described here?
'The great quantity of plants which Mr. Banks and Dr. Solander collected in this place induced me to give it the name of _____'

> **FASCINATING FACT: While in uncharted waters on 11th June 1770, HMS *Endeavour* struck the Great Barrier Reef. The crew frantically threw equipment, including all but four cannons, overboard to lighten the ship which was successfully refloated, but a hole had opened up in the hull. Midshipman Jonathan Monkhouse saved the day, fashioning a protective seal with a sail containing rope fibres. This was drawn under the ship, with the pressure of water forcing it into the hole to plug the leak.**

12TH GREATEST BRITON

James Cook was named number 12 in the BBC's *100 Greatest Britons*. Can you guess the others from the clues, including three famous explorers?

1. Prime Minister and Nobel Prize winner

2. Engineer known for building important bridges and tunnels

3. Royal, celebrated for her charity work

4. Naturalist, who went on a five-year voyage aboard HMS *Beagle*

5. Francis Bacon? Christopher Marlowe? Edward de Vere?

6. Scientist who gives his name to the unit of measure for force

7. Last of the Tudors

8. Formed the band the Quarrymen in 1956

9. Stands 169ft high over Westminster

10. Lord Protector of the Commonwealth

11. Explorer known for his *Endurance*

TRIVIA: NASA named the fifth and final operational space shuttle *Endeavour*, built between 1987 and 1992, after the ship Cook took on the first of his voyages of discovery. The third space shuttle, *Discovery*, built between 1979 and 1984 was named for both HMS *Discovery*, the ship Cook took on his third voyage, and *Discovery*, commanded by navigator Henry Hudson (*c*.1565–1611) who explored Canada and the northeastern USA.

CARSTEN NIEBUHR

A CONSCIENTIOUS
EXPLORER

Carsten Niebuhr (1733–1815) was a German-born traveller and surveyor, who was selected to join the Royal Danish Arabia Expedition (1761–1767) to Egypt, Arabia, Yemen and Syria – a part of the world practically unknown to Europeans. The party travelled to Constantinople and on to Egypt where they stayed for a year before travelling along the coast of the Red Sea, visiting Jeddah. From here, they travelled on to Sana'a, the capital of Yemen, where they were received by the Imam, who provided camels so they could make the journey southwards to Mocha. All of the men were stricken by malaria and two died in Mocha.

Late in 1763, the remaining travellers boarded a British vessel bound for Bombay but Niebuhr was the only one to survive, the others succumbing to malaria. After a long recuperation, Niebuhr explored Persia, Cyprus, Jerusalem and Turkey, before returning overland to Denmark in November 1767. His skilled observations and precise cartography led to the publication of his book *Travels Through Arabia and Other Countries in the East*, which was still being used a century later by travellers to the region.

> **FASCINATING FACT:** He was the only member of the party to truly adapt to his surroundings, eating and dressing like a local and learning how to communicate as an equal with the Arabs, offering them kindness and empathy. He even replaced his Danish servant with a Muslim guide because of the local man's knowledge, and for a time changed his own name to Abdullah, believing that 'the true observer is always a person who has lost his own identity'.

Match the letters with their correct geographical location to plot the journey Carsten Niebuhr took, starting in February 1761. We've marked the start and end of the journey for you.

_____	Cyprus	_____	Alexandria
_____	Bombay	_____	Warsaw
A,W	Copenhagen	_____	Jerusalem
_____	Basra	_____	Cairo
_____	Jeddah	_____	Shiraz
_____	Aleppo	_____	Sana'a
_____	Constantinople	_____	Muscat
_____	Suez	_____	Mosul
_____	Marseille	_____	Baghdad
_____	Bucharest	_____	Mocha

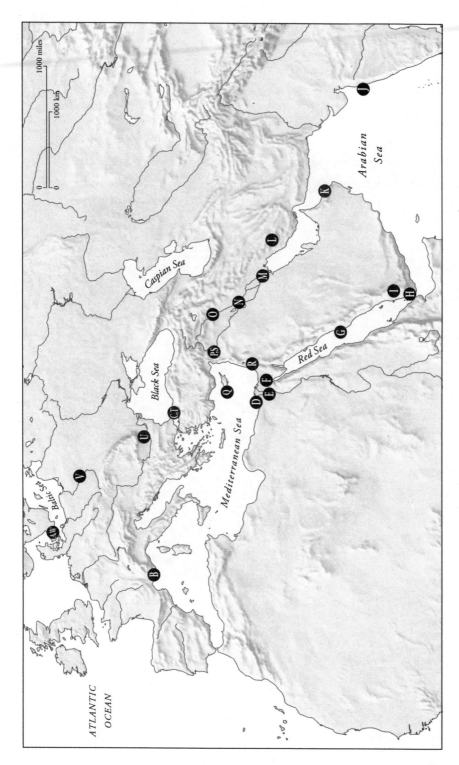

JEAN-FRANÇOIS DE GALAUP, COMTE DE LA PÉROUSE

THE LOST EXPLORER OF THE PACIFIC

Jean-François de Galaup (1741–1788), Comte de La Pérouse, was a French naval officer and navigator who, in 1785, was appointed by Louis XVI to lead a scientific expedition around the world.

His team departed from Brest in August 1785 with two vessels, *L'Astrolabe* and *La Boussole*, and sailed around South America and on to Easter Island. From here they travelled up the west coast of South America and on to North America, unsuccessfully attempting to find the fabled western entrance to the Northwest Passage. La Pérouse proceeded to the Philippines, then along the coastlines of Japan and Korea. He reached Botany Bay in modern-day Australia on 26th January 1788 and set sail for New Caledonia on 10th March, but subsequently disappeared in a naval mystery that rivalled the disappearance of Sir John Franklin. Then, in 1826, Irish sea captain Peter Dillon found several artefacts on the coral atoll of Vanikoro which were positively identified as belonging to *L'Astrolabe*. It seems both vessels had been wrecked on Vanikoro's reefs, where the surviving crew members had fashioned a small boat and disappeared into the unknown.

The map opposite of La Pérouse's route includes names for lands or regions that have since changed. Can you provide the modern-day names for the following islands?

1. Formosa

2. Sandwich Islands

3. Friendly Isles

4. Otaheite

5. Navigator Islands

6. New Hebrides

7. Which modern-day province of Canada, whose capital is Winnipeg, is marked as New South Wales?

FASCINATING FACT: One of the men who applied to join La Pérouse's voyage was a 16-year-old Corsican second lieutenant by the name of Napoléon Bonaparte, but his application was rejected.

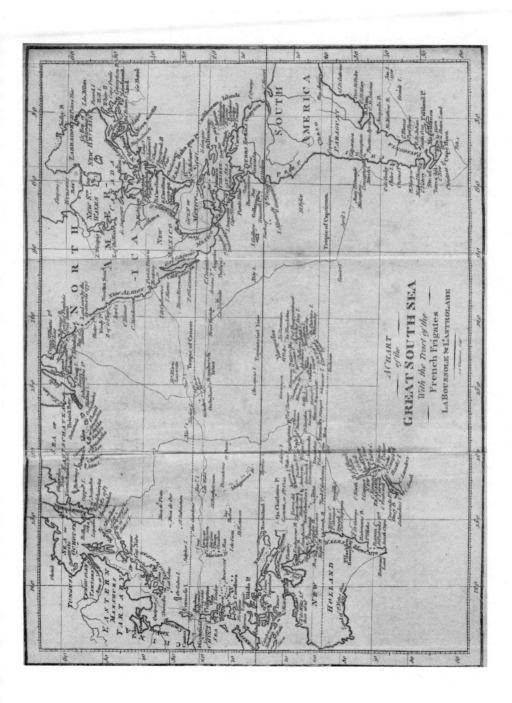

A CHART of the
GREAT SOUTH SEA
With the Tract of the
French Frigates
La BOUSSOLE & L'ASTROLABE

67

ALEXANDER VON HUMBOLDT

'THE GREATEST SCIENTIFIC TRAVELLER WHO EVER LIVED'

Alexander von Humboldt (1769–1859) was a German naturalist and explorer, and one of the most influential scientists of the 18th and 19th centuries. He displayed a keen interest in the sciences from a young age, earning him the nickname of the 'little apothecary'. While studying at the University of Göttingen, he immersed himself in geology, and divided his time between exploring mines and finding and classifying plants. During his subsequent employment as a Prussian mining official, von Humboldt developed a safety lamp and a respirator. In 1797, he finally committed his life to scientific exploration and, in 1799, he was granted permission by the King of Spain to travel to South America. A man of means with a significant estate inherited after the death of his mother, von Humboldt was able to finance the five-year-long expedition himself.

Can you spot the true statements below?

1. Alexander von Humboldt was the first person to describe the phenomenon and cause of human-induced climate change in 1800.

2. Alexander von Humboldt was the first person to describe the phenomenon and cause of hurricanes in 1800.

3. Alexander von Humboldt invented the term 'isotherms' to describe the connections between different geographical points around the world experiencing the same temperature.

4. Alexander von Humboldt invented the term 'magnetic storms' to refer to disturbances in the Earth's magnetic field.

5. Alexander von Humboldt was a cavalry officer in the West Prussian Dragoons regiment, which seized Napoleon Bonaparte's carriage at the Battle of Waterloo in 1815.

6. In April 1827, Alexander von Humboldt spent 40 minutes at the bottom of the River Thames river in the diving bell used by the British engineer Isambard Kingdom Brunel during the construction of the Thames Tunnel.

> **FASCINATING FACT:** In 1802, von Humboldt climbed Ecuador's Chimborazo, reaching a height of 20,702 feet (6,310 metres) before encountering an impassable crevasse. He later correctly identified that the lack of oxygen in the air at great heights was the reason behind altitude sickness.

A PIONEERING VOYAGE

The five-year-long expedition that von Humboldt undertook from 1799 to 1804, accompanied by French botanist Aimé Bonpland (1773–1858), wound its way through Venezuela, Cuba, Colombia, Ecuador, Peru and Mexico. Von Humboldt gathered together the most advanced scientific equipment he could lay his hands on, for he planned to measure everything, from atmospheric pressure to ocean temperature; terrestrial magnetism and humidity to the distribution of animals and plants. They would face extreme hardship, including an outbreak of typhoid fever aboard their ship, an encounter with electric eels in the Orinoco river, which claimed the lives of several horses, and the constant torment of mosquitoes.

The extraordinary findings of this journey, including a collection of around 3,600 plants that were unknown to science at the time, were published over a 21-year period, which established von Humboldt as one of the most influential scientists in history. Among his towering achievements, this expedition laid the foundations for biogeography as a subject and the modern concept of geography.

Which animals or plants is von Humboldt describing?

1. 'At the spot where the bushes were thickest, our horses were frightened by the yell of an animal that seemed to follow us closely. It was a large _____, which had roamed for three years among these mountains.'(CLUE: luxury car brand)

2. 'A courageous bird, the intelligence of which is developed like that of our domestic ravens.' (CLUE: known for its distinctive bill)

3. 'These animals, as large as our pigs, have no weapons of defence; they swim somewhat better than they run: yet they become the prey of the crocodiles in the water, and of the tigers on land.' (CLUE: largest living rodent)

4. 'This appearance of sterility is here attributed, as it is everywhere in the valleys of Aragua, to the cultivation of _____; which, according to the planters, is, of all plants, that which most exhausts the ground.' (CLUE: dye)

5. 'The missionary, who accompanied us, had his fever-fit on him. In order to quench the thirst by which he was tormented, the idea suggested itself to us of preparing a refreshing beverage for him in one of the excavations of the rock. We had taken on board at Atures an

Indian basket called a mapire, filled with sugar, limes,
and those grenadillas, or fruits of the _____,
to which the Spaniards give the name of parchas.'
(CLUE: exotic flowering plant connected to Christian
theology)

AN ENLIGHTENED FRIENDSHIP

After spending over a year in New Spain (Mexico), von
Humboldt travelled to the United States of America in 1804,
securing an invitation from President Thomas Jefferson (1743–
1826) to visit him at the White House. Von Humboldt was in
a unique position to provide Jefferson with information about
the military strength, population and trade of New Spain
(Mexico), which was now a neighbouring country, following the
Louisiana Purchase in December the previous year. Such was
von Humboldt's fame in the US, that cities across the country
commemorated the 100th anniversary of von Humboldt's birth
and a bust of his head was unveiled in New York's Central Park.

**Ten of the states in the USA feature towns or counties
named after von Humboldt. Can you name them from the
clues below?**

1. The state Barack Obama represented as senator

2. State of Mount Rushmore, previously one larger
   territory that was split in two

3. Tornado Alley state whose largest city is Omaha

4. The only state name that starts with two vowels

5. The home of Jack Daniel's

6. The geographic centre of the United States of America

7. The 'Land of 10,000 Lakes' with a baseball team named the 'Twins'

8. Home of the Grand Canyon

9. The largest living tree resides here

10. Well known for its connection to gambling

FASCINATING FACT: More species have been named in Alexander von Humboldt's honour than anyone else in history. In total, almost 300 plants and 100 animals have been named after him, including the South American Humboldt penguin and the large, aggressive Humboldt squid.

Right: Ecuador's Chimborazo.
Plate from 'Atlas geographique et physique des régions équinxiales du Nouveau Continent', 1814–1834 by Alexander von Humboldt.

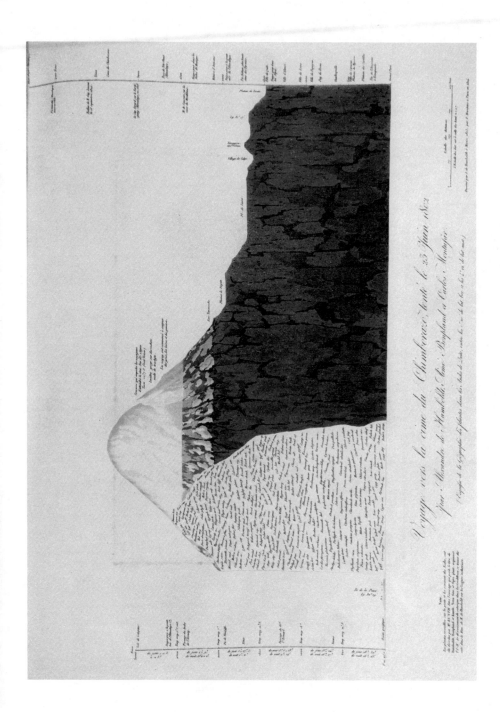

75

MERIWETHER LEWIS AND WILLIAM CLARK

HEROES OF THE AMERICAN WEST

Meriwether Lewis (1774–1809) and William Clark (1770–1838) undertook the first American expedition to reach the Pacific coast. The Louisiana Purchase of 1803 effectively doubled the land area of the United States of America, and President Thomas Jefferson commissioned an expedition, primarily to explore and exploit the trade potential of their new territory. The party set out in May 1804 and returned to St Louis after two years, four months and ten days. They were joined by a young Shoshone Indian woman called Sacagawea, who played a vital role translating and securing diplomatic connections with Native American populations. The 8,000-mile-long expedition was a huge success, producing invaluable maps, establishing peaceful trade connections, and collecting hundreds of animal and plant specimens.

Lewis and Clark visited 11 modern-day American states on their journey to the Pacific. Can you work out the names of the states from the cryptic clues?

1. Unwell, ninth letter make a racket

2. A young lady feels resentful until she adds a pronoun

3. Misspelled container of elite British troops

4. Jupiterian moon joins an abbreviated Antipodean State

5. Originally called, an undergarment, a blemish

6. Meridional, Russian affirmative, in fixed quantities

7. The flip side of the clue above

8. Gallic peak welcomes a leather maker

9. Freudian unconscious meets an ancient gardening tool

10. The rocks have vanished!

11. That pile of laundry weighs a huge amount

Can you guess the name of the animal from the description in Lewis and Clark's journals?

1. 'This animal is the largest of the Carnivorous kind I ever Saw we had nothing that could way him, I think his weight may be Stated at 500 pounds, he measured 8 feet 71/2 In. from his nose to the extremity of the Toe.'

   A: Black Bear   B: Grizzly Bear
   C: Mountain Lion (Cougar)

2. '. . . like a Dog with its ears Cut off, his tale and hair like that of a Ground hog . . . his Skin thick & loose, white & hair Short under its belly, of the Species of the Bear, and it has a white Streake from its nose to its Sholders...[sic]'

   A: Raccoon   B: Skunk   C: American Badger

3. 'They generally associate in large societies placing their burrows near each other and frequently occupy in this manner several hundred acres of land. when at rest above ground their position is generally erect on their hinder feet and rump; thus they will generally set and bark at you as you approach them, their note being much that of the little toy dogs, their yelps are in quick succession and at each they a motion to their tails upwards.'

   A: Prairie Dog   B: Groundhog   C: Meerkat

4. 'In returning through the level bottom of Medecine river and about 200 yards distant from the Missouri, my direction led me directly to an anamal [sic] that I at first supposed was a wolf. But on nearer approach or about sixty paces distant I discovered that it was not. Its colour was a brownish yellow; it was standing near it's burrow, and when I approached it thus nearly, it couched itself down like a cat looking immediately at me as if it designed to spring on me.'

   A: Wolverine   B: Honey Badger   C: Coyote

5. 'The beak is a whiteish yellow the under part connected to a bladder like pouch, this pouch is connected to both sides of the lower beak and extends down on the under side of the neck and terminates in the stomach—this pouch is uncovered with feathers, and is formed two skins the one on the inner and the other on the center side a small quantity of flesh and strings of which the anamal [sic] has at pleasure the power of moving or drawing in such manner as to contract it at pleasure. In the present subject I measured this pouch and found its contents 5 gallons of water'

   A: Wood Stork   B: American White Pelican
   C: King Penguin

THE ROYAL GEOGRAPHICAL SOCIETY COLLECTIONS

QUIZ 1

With over two million documents, maps, photographs, paintings, periodicals, artefacts and books, the Society's Collections span 500 years of geography, travel and exploration. From Inuit boots from the Canadian Arctic to ceremonial leopard claws from the then Belgian Congo, it is a wonderful treasure trove of the most cherished artefacts and personal belongings from some of the world's greatest expeditions.

In these pages you can put your knowledge of these incredible items to the test with the Royal Geographical Society Collections Quiz! Navigate the Roman settlements found on Ptolemy's pioneering cartography; trace the four routes of the great Christopher Columbus; tag along with John C. Frémont as he traverses the mountainous regions of the American West; and work out which Arctic creatures Nordenskiöld is describing during the first successful circumnavigation of Eurasia.

It's time to dust off your snow boots and retrieve your compass for the adventure ahead. Good luck and safe journey!

PTOLEMY

PIONEERING POLYMATH

Claudius Ptolemaeus (Ptolemy) (*c.* AD 100–170) was a Greco-Roman scholar who wrote groundbreaking treatises on astronomy, mathematics and geography. One of his major contributions to geography was to record latitudes and longitudes for approximately 8,000 places. While none of his original maps have been recovered, the geographical information he gathered survives and was used in the Middle Ages to reconstruct maps of the known world during the Roman Empire.

FASCINATING FACT: For over 1,400 years, the prevailing astronomical model of the universe, with Earth at the centre, was created by Ptolemy, and was later known as the Ptolemaic System. It was only superseded in 1543 by the heliocentric (Sun-centred) Copernican System proposed by Nicolaus Copernicus.

This map of the British Isles was created in 1486 from information contained in a Ptolemaic atlas. The fact that Scotland is rotated roughly 90° clockwise at the point of Hadrian's Wall is most likely attributed to a lack of land data and the reliance on naval accounts which would have been blighted by rough seas and strong currents.

Some of the Roman settlements marked on the map were located on sites that have become the following English cities – can you find them?

London

Bath

Winchester

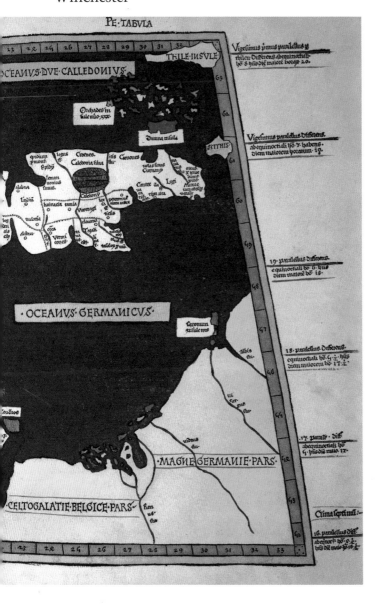

IBN BATTUTA

THE GREATEST TRAVELLER
WHO LIVED?

Ibn Battuta (1304–*c*.1368) was a Muslim explorer born in 1304 in Tangier into a family of legal scholars. He journeyed the length and breadth of the Muslim world and beyond over a period of 30 years. During the course of his travels, Ibn Battuta visited at least 40 modern-day countries.

In all, Battuta completed seven pilgrimages to Mecca, endured a shipwreck, battled several malignant fevers and survived a devastating plague outbreak, yet he is overshadowed by the other great explorer of the medieval period, Marco Polo. Battuta travelled much farther than Polo, visiting Arabia, India and trans-Saharan Africa.

> **FASCINATING FACT: In all, Ibn Battuta covered about 75,000 miles, which is commonly believed to be the farthest anybody travelled before the age of steam.**

Can you match the names of the (present-day) Countries that Ibn Battuta visited during his travels with their flags?

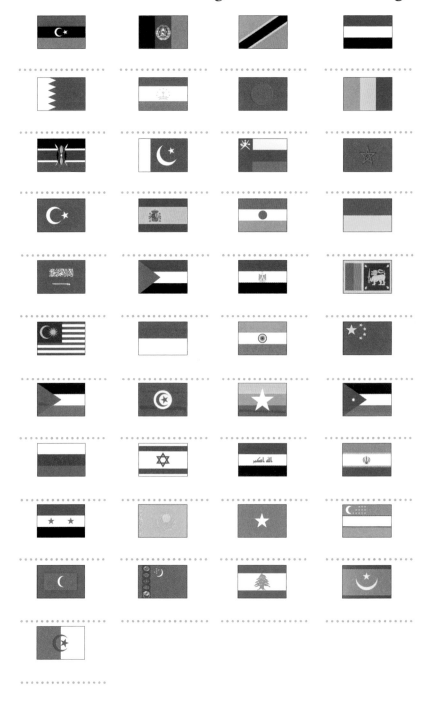

Morocco	Tanzania
Algeria	Ukraine
Tunisia	Russia
Libya	Kazakhstan
Spain	Turkmenistan
Egypt	Uzbekistan
Palestine	Tajikistan
Israel	Afghanistan
Jordan	India
Lebanon	Pakistan
Syria	Maldives
Turkey	Sri Lanka
Saudi Arabia	Bangladesh
Yemen	China
Oman	Indonesia
Bahrain	Mali
Iraq	Mauritania
Iran	Niger
Sudan	Myanmar
Somalia	Malaysia
Kenya	

Which six famous ancient cities is Ibn Battuta describing?

1. 'It is said that in _____ there are twelve thousand water-carriers who transport water on camels, and thirty thousand hirers of mules and donkeys, and that on its Nile there are thirty-six thousand vessels belong to the Sultan and his subjects…'

   A: Tripoli   B: Jerusalem   C: Cairo

2. 'I left Tangier, my birthplace, on Thursday, 2nd Rajab, 725 [14th June, 1325], being at that time twenty-two lunar years of age, with the intention of making the Pilgrimage to the Holy House at Mecca and the Tomb of the Prophet at_____'

   A: Jerusalem   B: Medina   C: Jedda

3. 'The baths at _____ are numerous and excellently constructed, most of them being painted with pitch, which has the appearance of black marble. This pitch is brought from a spring between Kufa and Basra, from which it flows continually.'

   A: Baghdad   B: Tehran   C: Kuwait City

4. 'The prosperity of Tunis was due solely to its advantageous position at the debouchment of the main trade routes from the interior, which made it the premier commercial city of the Maghrib and second only to _____ among the Muslim Mediterranean ports.'

   A: Fez   B: Khartoum   C: Alexandria

5. 'The city is enormous in size, and in two parts separated by a great river [the Golden Horn], in which there is a rising and ebbing tide. In former times there was a stone bridge over it, but it fell into ruins and the crossing is now made in boats.'

A: Delhi   B: Constantinople   C: Tripoli

6. 'On the next day we arrived at the city of _____ the metropolis of India, a vast and magnificent city, uniting beauty with strength. It is surrounded by a wall that has no equal in the world, and is the largest city in India, nay rather the largest city in the entire Muslim Orient.'

A: Calcutta   B: Bombay   C: Delhi

Created shortly after the death of Ibn Battuta, *The Catalan Atlas* (of 1375) is thought to depict Battula travelling to meet Mansa Musa, ruler of the Mali empire from 1312 to his death in 1357, thought to be one of the richest people of all time.

CHRISTOPHER COLUMBUS

FOUR VOYAGES OF DISCOVERY

Christopher Columbus (*c.*1451–1506) famously made four voyages of discovery, the success of which triggered numerous European expeditions across the Atlantic, Indian and Pacific Oceans to trade, conquer and colonise lands occupied by indigenous people. While Columbus established the first European settlement in the Americas, he also helped to bring about the trade in people to work in mines and plantations constructed by colonists.

Funded by King Ferdinand and Queen Isabella of Spain, Columbus set sail on his first voyage in August 1492 with a fleet of three ships – the flagship *Santa Maria*, the *Pinta* and the *Niña*. He planned to head west, believing that China would be the first land he sighted in a matter of weeks.

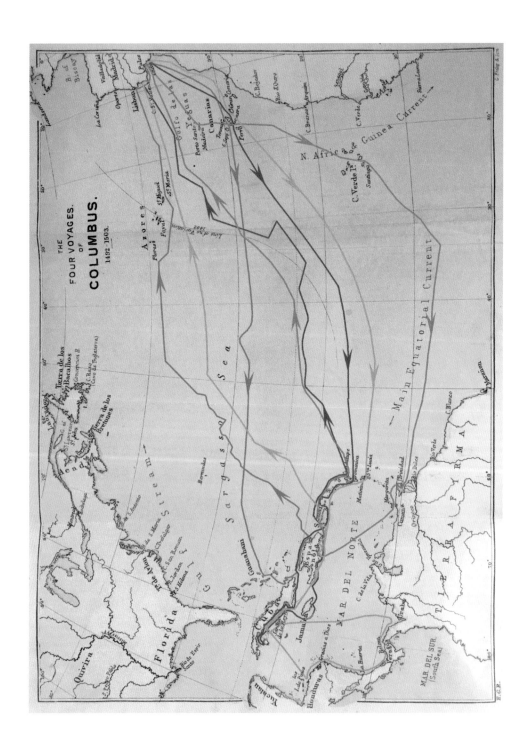

THE
FOUR VOYAGES.
OF
COLUMBUS.
1492-1503.

Can you identify which voyage is which on the map from the clues below?

First Voyage: Columbus sails to the north of an island that shares its name with his flagship.

Second Voyage: Includes a visit to an island named for a day of the week.

Third Voyage: Columbus fulfils his vow to name first island sighted for the Father, Son and Holy Ghost.

Fourth Voyage: Weather suddenly calms during a severe storm while rounding a cape, so Columbus names it in gratitude to heavens.

MISCALCULATIONS AND MISJUDGEMENTS

Columbus made some extraordinary discoveries, but he also made some remarkable miscalculations and misjudgements, such as believing he had reached China when he sighted Cuba. Can you spot which answer is true?

1. Against the advice of astronomy and navigational experts at the time and the works of Greek mathematician Eratosthenes, who had estimated the circumference of the Earth fairly accurately in 240 BC, Columbus attempted his own calculation. Approximately how far was he off by?

   A: 1,000 miles   B: 3,000 miles   C: 4,500 miles

2. Again, contrary to the prevailing wisdom at the time that the Earth was round, Columbus likened the shape of the Earth to which fruit?

   A: Pear   B: Lemon   C: Avocado

3. Which hitherto mythological creature did Columbus believe he saw, describing it as 'not half as beautiful as they are painted'.

   A: Nymph   B: Mermaid   C: Siren

4. On Christmas Eve 1492, Columbus, having been awake for 48 hours, decided to take some rest below in his cabin on the *Santa Maria*. He left his sailing master in charge, who, against strict instructions from his captain, also decided to rest, leaving the ship's wheel in the hands of the cabin boy. What happened next?

   A: The *Santa Maria* hit an abandoned ship, tearing a hole in its side and causing its evacuation to the nearby ship *La Niña* before the *Santa Maria* sank.

   B: The *Santa Maria* was carried by ocean currents towards land, running aground on a sandbank and sinking the following afternoon.

   C: The *Santa Maria* was ambushed by a Portuguese warship. Columbus managed to lose his adversary in a sea mist but the *Santa Maria* sank the following day.

6. 'In the early part of the day two of our men fired on a panther, a little below our encampment, and wounded it; they informed us that it was very large, had just killed a deer partly devoured it, and in the act of concealing the balance [sic] as they discovered him.'

A: Jaguar   B: Lynx   C: Mountain Lion (Cougar)

FASCINATING FACT: Lewis invited Clark to join the Corps of Discovery in 1803. Lewis had been commissioned earlier that year to explore the newly purchased territory of Louisiana by President Thomas Jefferson who described the aims of the expedition as being 'To explore the Missouri River and such principal stream of it as by its course and communication with the waters of the Pacific (make). . . the most direct and practicable water communication across this continent.'

IDA PFEIFFER

A WOMAN'S JOURNEY AROUND
THE WORLD

Ida Pfeiffer (1797–1858) was an intrepid Austrian explorer who undertook two trips around the world, collecting many plant and insect specimens along the way. She was one of the first female travellers and became the first woman to be granted honorary member status at the geographical societies of Paris and Berlin. She wrote several books about her various adventures, which were translated into multiple languages.

On her first expedition in 1846, she travelled to Greece, Asia Minor, Persia, China, India, Brazil, Argentina, Chile and Tahiti. On her second expedition, she reached Australia, Peru, Ecuador and California and became one of the first people to write about the Batak people of northern Sumatra.

Which remarkable man-made wonders is Ida describing?

1. 'Sta. Maria ad Martyres, or the Rotunda, once the _____ of Agrippa, is in better preservation than any other monument of ancient Rome. The interior is almost in its pristine condition; it contains no less than fifteen altars. In this church Raphael is buried. The Rotunda has no windows, but receives air and light through a circular opening in the cupola.'

2. '. . . a statue of most colossal dimensions, situated at no great distance from the great pyramid, is so covered with sand that only the head and a small portion of the bust remain visible. The head alone is twenty-two feet in height.'

3. '_____ is without doubt the most remarkable city of its kind that exists. A great portion of the town is surrounded by walls, and entire rows of houses, several temples, the theatre, the forum, in short a vast number of buildings, streets, and squares lay open before

us . . . The deserted aspect of this town had a very melancholy effect in my eyes. Though a great portion of the town has already been dug out, only three hundred skeletons have been found – a proof that the greater portion of the inhabitants effected their escape.'

4. 'Shortly afterwards we came near the hill on which the beautiful _____ stands. I gazed for a long time on all that was to be seen; the statues of the Grecian heroes, the history of the country came back to my mind; and I glowed with desire to set my foot on the land which, from my earliest childhood, had appeared to me, after Rome and Jerusalem, as the most interesting in the earth.'

5. 'The monument stands in the centre of a garden, upon an open terrace of red sandstone, raised twelve feet above the ground. It represents a mosque of an octagon form, with lofty arched entrances, which, together with the four minarets that stand at the corners of the terrace, is entirely built of white marble. The principal dome rises to a height of 260 feet, and is surrounded by four smaller ones.

6. 'I sat down before the pictures in mosaic, underneath the huge dome and the canopy; then I stood before the statues and monuments, and could only gaze in wonder at every thing. The expense of building and decorating this church is said to have amounted to 45,852,000 dollars. It occupies the site of Nero's circus. Two arcades, with four rows of pillars and ninety-six statues, surround the square leading to the church.'

7. 'The city walls are described as having been 150 feet high, and twenty feet thick. The city was defended by 250 towers; it was closed by a hundred brazen gates, and its circumference was sixty miles. It was separated into two parts by the Euphrates. On each bank stood a beautiful palace, and the two were united by an artistic bridge, and even a tunnel was constructed by the Queen Semiramis. But the greatest curiosities were the temples of Belus and the _____. . . ascribed to Nebuchadnezar [sic], who is said to have built them at the wish of his wife Amytis.'

Which geographical features is Ida describing?

1. 'This voyage was one of the most beautiful... The traveller continually sees the most charming landscapes of blooming Sicily; and at Syracuse we can already descry on a clear day the giant _____ rearing its head 10,000 feet above the level of the sea.'

2. '. . . it may rather be termed an oblong lake, shut in by mountains, than a sea. Not the slightest sign of life can be detected in the water; not a ripple disturbs its sleeping surface. A boat of any kind is of course quite out of the question.'

3. 'At the particular desire of Herr M., who was well acquainted with all the remarkable points about the volcano, our guide now led the way to the so-called "hell", a little crater which formed itself it in the year 1834. To reach it we had to climb about over fields of lava for half an hour . . . The lava is of different colours, according as it has been exposed to the atmosphere for a longer or a shorter period. The oldest lava has the hue of granite, and almost its hardness, for which reasons it is largely used for building houses and paving streets.'

4. 'On the 22nd of December, we passed the remarkable mountain scenery of Junghera, which rises, like an island of rocks, from the majestic _____. This spot was, in former times, looked on as the holiest in the whole course of the river.'

5. 'In the evening, at about seven o'clock, we arrived at Pest. The magnificent houses, or rather palaces, skirting the left bank of the _____, and the celebrated ancient fortress and town of Ofen on the right, form a splendid spectacle.'

6. 'Here the mighty _____, which irrigates the whole country with the hundreds of canals cut from its banks through every region, divides itself into two principal branches, one of which falls into the sea at Rosetta, and the other at Damietta.'

7. 'It seemed, from its magnitude, as if separated from the other mountains, and standing alone; but it is in fact, connected with the chain of Taurus by a low range of hills. Its highest summit is divided in such a way that between two peaks there is a small plain, on which it is said that Noah's ark was left after the deluge. There are people who affirm that it would still be found there if the snow could be removed.'

Right: Frontipiece from *A Woman's journey round the world* by Ida Pfeiffer, 1852.

A Woman's Journey Round the World.

CAPE HORN.

OFFICE OF THE NATIONAL ILLUSTRATED LIBRARY,
227 STRAND.

JAMES CLARK ROSS

POLAR PIONEER

James Clark Ross (1800–1862) was a British naval officer and explorer. He joined the Royal Navy in 1812 before accompanying his uncle Sir John Ross (1777–1856), a hero of the Napoleonic Wars and a polar explorer, on his first expedition to find the Northwest Passage in 1818. On Sir John's second Arctic expedition, James famously led a party that located the North Magnetic Pole. He was given command of his own Antarctic expedition between 1839 and 1843, sailing the ships HMS *Erebus* and HMS *Terror*. Ross discovered the Ross Sea and a region of Antarctica he named Victoria Land. The largest ice shelf in Antarctica, which Ross initially called 'The Barrier', was renamed the Ross Ice Shelf in his honour in 1953.

In 1848, Ross led an expedition to find Sir John Franklin, the explorer and Royal Navy officer who mysteriously disappeared while trying to chart the Northwest Passage in 1847. Ross devised a novel method of fitting inscribed copper collars on captured Arctic fox cubs, giving the location of Ross' flagship the HMS *Enterprise* in case they found their way to Franklin's camp scavenging for food. Ross' expedition was ultimately unsuccessful, as were the 25 other expeditions in search of Franklin undertaken between 1847 and 1859. It was only in 2014 that the wreckage of Franklin's lost expedition was found.

Copper collar fastened on neck of fox cub caught and released by staff of HMS *Enterprise*, at Port Leopold on the far northeast corner of Somerset Island, 1848.

FASCINATING FACT: The wreck of HMS *Erebus* was finally discovered in September 2014 and the remains of HMS *Terror* were found in September 2016. They have both been designated National Historic Sites of Canada.

Can you find the coordinates of the North Magnetic Pole that James Clark Ross found on 31st May 1831 by answering the questions below?

1. To find the latitude measurement in degrees, add together the number of stars on the following flags: United States of America, Europe, Australia, Ghana and Vietnam

2. To find the latitude measurement in minutes, add together the number of stripes on the following flags: Nigeria and Poland

3. To find the longitude measurement in degrees, work out the number of USA states beginning with 'N' multiplied by the number of sovereign states in South America

4. To find the longitude measurement in minutes, work out the number of Canadian provinces multiplied by the number of countries in Africa beginning with 'B' plus the number of countries that border Switzerland, plus the number of flags that feature a gun

---

FASCINATING FACT: The North Magnetic Pole changes location over time due to changes in the Earth's spinning molten iron and nickel core. In the mid-1900s, it was only moving around 100ft a day (equivalent to 6.9 miles a year), but by 2000 it was shifting approximately 34 miles a year.

THE ARCTIC EXPLORATION

The fate of Sir John Franklin's expedition and the names of his ships (which were originally used by Sir James Clark Ross) have been immortalised in works of literature and the naming of geographical features.

Can you guess the Arctic connections from these clues?

1. Two Antarctic volcanoes were named after the ships HMS *Erebus* and HMS *Terror*, which the fictional Captain Nemo references in which famous adventure novel?

2. Franklin's ships are mentioned in which classic novella of 1899 by Joseph Conrad about a voyage up the Congo river?

3. Which adventurous Monty Python member wrote a book about HMS *Erebus* that was published in 2018?

4. The fate of the Franklin expedition inspired the play *The Frozen Deep*, written by Wilkie Collins and which author, who went by the occasional pseudonym Boz?

5. Which American author, born Samuel Langhorne Clemens, satirised the fate of the Franklin expedition in *Some Learned Fables for Good Old Boys and Girls* (1875)?

6. Erebus is the name of a crater on which planet that was visited by NASA's Opportunity rover in 2005?

7. Named after Ross' flagship, Mount Erebus is the second-highest volcano in Antarctica. What is the name of the highest?

In March 1842, HMS *Erebus* was forced to turn across the path of HMS *Terror* to avoid an iceberg and the two ships collided. The rigging of the two ships was entangled until eventually *Erebus* broke free.

DAVID LIVINGSTONE

MAN ON A MISSION

David Livingstone (1813–1873) was a Scottish physician, missionary and explorer who became the first European to explore many parts of Africa. Despite, aged 10, working 14-hour days in a cotton mill, he attended school in the evenings and worked hard to become a medical missionary.

He travelled to Africa for the first time in 1841, co-founding a mission at Mabotsa, in South Africa. His motto became 'Christianity, Commerce and Civilization' with a mission to help abolish the slave trade and replace it with commercial alternatives, such as agriculture. The key to this, he believed, was to navigate the Zambezi river to make use of the interior of the continent. He would later become obsessed with finding the source of the River Nile – one of the great quests of scientific exploration in the Victorian era.

Unfortunately, Livingstone's timeline is completely out of order. Answer the trivia question at the top of each box to find the correct sequence. It continues on the next page!

| | **The number of points on the Star of David** |

Livingstone leads a second expedition to Africa, attempting to open up the Zambezi river to navigation and exploit the potential for commercial agriculture. Tragically, his wife Mary died of malaria four years in to the expedition. Despite becoming the first Europeans to reach Lake Malawi, the expedition was not a success, with the Zambezi deemed 'unnavigable'.

| | **The number of moons orbiting Mars** |

Livingstone marries Mary Moffat, the daughter of Scottish missionary Robert Moffat who had inspired Livingstone to direct his missionary work in Africa.

| | **The highest category of hurricane** |

Livingstone makes a journey across Africa, from Luanda on the Atlantic coast to Quelimane on the Indian Ocean. He was the first European to do so at that latitude.

☐ The number of bits in a byte

Welsh explorer Henry Morton Stanley is charged with locating Livingstone after very little had been heard of him for six years. He finally finds him near Lake Tanganyika, uttering the famous but possibly apocryphal greeting: 'Doctor Livingstone, I presume?'

☐ The atomic number of hydrogen

In the village of Mabotsa, South Africa, lions had attacked villagers and their livestock. Livingstone understood that killing one lion would cause the pride to move on. He wounded a male lion, but had not injured it sufficiently to prevent it springing upon him, breaking his arm and leaving 11 teeth wounds before the lion succumbed to its injuries.

☐ The number sitting below the '&' sign on a UK and US keyboard

Livingstone is tasked with confirming the source of the Nile, after two rival Nile explorers were locked in disagreement. John Hanning Speke (correctly) believed the source was Lake Victoria, while Richard Francis Burton was convinced it was Lake Tanganyika. In the end, Livingstone believed it to be a third option: the Lualaba river.

□ **The number of sculptures of former presidents carved into Mount Rushmore**

Travelling along the Zambezi river, Livingstone reaches a huge series of waterfalls named Mosi-oa-tunya (the smoke that thunders) by the Kololo people. He is the first European to see it, naming it after Queen Victoria. He remarks: '... scenes so lovely must have been gazed upon by angels in their flight.'

□ **The most number of times any city has hosted the Summer Olympic Games**

Livingstone reaches Lake Ngami after crossing the Kalahari Desert. He writes an account of his journey to the London Missionary Society, who pass it to the Royal Geographical Society, who in turn award him their Founder's Medal.

HALL OF HEROES

The National Wallace Monument overlooking Stirling in Scotland was erected in 1869 to commemorate Sir William Wallace. Inside are 16 busts of legendary Scottish figures, known as the Hall of Heroes. **Livingstone is one of the heroes, but can you name the others from the clues?**

1. Arachnid spinning a web

2. Supper on 25th January

3. Free-market pioneer

4. Famous Scottish station named in honour of one of his novels

5. Bright spark who gave his name to a unit of power

6. Deep thinker with a surname sounding like the county town of Cumbria

ISABELLA BIRD

PIONEERING ADVENTURER

Isabella Bird (1831–1904) was a groundbreaking explorer, writer and photographer. After undergoing an operation to remove a spinal tumour in 1850, her doctor recommended travel as a means to help her recuperate. Her destination was North America and the letters she wrote home formed the content of her first book *The Englishwoman in America* (1856). She travelled to Australia then Hawaii in 1872, climbing both Mauna Loa and Mauna Kea before exploring the Rocky Mountains of Colorado. In 1878, she travelled extensively around Japan, becoming the first Englishwoman to do so before exploring China, Singapore and Malaya. She died aged 72, while planning another trip to China. She was a prolific and impassioned writer, cataloguing all of her adventures, critiquing the ill-treatment of women and describing many places poorly understood in Western Europe.

Can you work out which book title goes with Isabella Bird's description of the country or area?

The Hawaiian Archipelago
Journeys in Persia and Kurdistan
Notes on Old Edinburgh
The Golden Chersonese and the Way Thither
Among the Tibetans
The Englishwoman in America
A Lady's Life in the Rocky Mountains
Unbeaten Tracks in Japan

1. 'It is the "happy hunting-ground" of the… sportsman and tourist, the resort of artists and invalids, the home of pashm shawls and exquisitely embroidered fabrics, and the land of Lalla Rookh.'

2. 'I decided to visit… attracted less by the reputed excellence of its climate than by the certainty that it possessed, in an especial degree, those sources of novel and sustained interest which conduce so essentially to the enjoyment and restoration of a solitary health-seeker. The climate disappointed me, but, though I found the country a study rather than a rapture, its interest exceeded my largest expectations.'

3. 'I have found a dream of beauty at which one might look all one's life and sigh. Not lovable, like the Sandwich Islands, but beautiful in its own way… snow-

splotched mountains, huge pines, red-woods, sugar
pines, silver spruce; a crystalline atmosphere, waves of
the richest color; and a pine-hung lake which mirrors
all beauty on its surface.'

4. 'There were lofty peaks, truly – grey and red, sun-
scorched and wind-bleached, glowing here and there
with traces of their fiery origin; but they were cleft
by deep chasms and ravines of cool shadow and
entrancing green, and falling water streaked their sides
– a most welcome vision after eleven months of the
desert sea and the dusty browns of Australia and New
Zealand.'

5. 'We know that they are famous for smoking,
spitting, "gouging", and bowie-knives—for monster
hotels, steamboat explosions, railway collisions, and
repudiated debts.'

6. 'A *shamal* or N.W. wind following on the sirocco
which had accompanied us up "the Gulf" was lashing
the shallow waters of the roadstead into reddish yeast
as we let go the anchor opposite the sea front of
Bushire...'

7. 'Canton and Saigon, and whatever else is comprised
in the second half of my title, are on one of the best
beaten tracks of travelers, and need no introductory
remarks.'

8. 'Over the din and discord of city sins, and over the wall of the city sorrows, came the sweet sounds of St Giles's bells announcing that the Sabbath had begun.'

FASCINATING FACT: In 1892, Isabella Bird became one of the first women to be elected a Fellow of the Royal Geographical Society. She had been awarded Honorary Fellowship of the Royal Scottish Geographical Society in 1890, became a member of the Royal Photographic Society in 1897 and was awarded the Royal Order of Kapiolani by the King of Hawaii in 1881.

See if you can find the answers to the crossword below based on Isabella Bird's adventures around the world.

ACROSS

6. Type of palm growing in tropical and subtropical regions of Asia associated with furniture-making and corporal punishment

7. Southeast-Asian port that was ceded to the East India Company by the Sultan of Johore in 1824

8. Traditional religion of Japan

10. Hawaiian greeting which Bird describes '... already represents to me all of kindness and goodwill that language can express.'

11. Popular term for a bandit of the Western USA in the 19th century

12. The largest of the active volcanoes of Hawaii, which Bird described as 'a burning mountain 13,750 feet high!'

DOWN

1. Anglicised Farsi term for a group of travellers

2. Divisive Southeast-Asian fruit that 'grows to the size of a man's head, and is covered closely with hard, sharp spines.'

3. Obsolete term for the Emperor of Japan but very much in use in the middle of the 18th century

4. Member of a Muslim religious order who has taken a vow of austerity; known for their wild rituals

5. Flower associated with the Emperor of Japan's imperial seat

9. American freshwater lake that Bird described as 'a dream of beauty at which one might look all one's life and sigh.'

FRIDTJOF NANSEN

FARTHEST NORTH

Fridtjof Nansen (1861–1930) was a Norwegian explorer and champion skier renowned for his contributions to polar exploration. In 1888, he became the first person to traverse Greenland on skis, earning him a gold medal from the Royal Geographical Society. Between 1893 and 1896, Nansen attempted to reach the geographic North Pole during the *Fram* expedition, falling short but travelling farther north than anyone in recorded history. Among his other achievements, the data he gathered during the *Fram* expedition provided new assessments of the geography and geology of the Arctic Circle.

Nansen employed revolutionary techniques during the *Fram* expedition, using a specially designed ship with a rounded hull to withstand the pack ice and drift along with the current. In contrast to previous explorers, Nansen called on Inuit and Sami expertise, using Sami sledges, Inuit shoes and learning the Inuit language.

Work out the latitude and longitude the following explorers reached on their quests to travel as far north as possible by solving the number puzzles below:

Date	Explorer(s)	Latitude	Longitude
1596	William Barentz		
1707	Cornelis Giles		n/a
1806	William Scoresby Sr		
1827	Sir William Edward Parry		
1875	Sir Albert Hastings Markham		
1882	Adolphus Greely		
1895	Fridtjof Nansen		

WILLIAM BARENTS

Latitude: HTTP code for 'Not Found' **divided by** the number of lions at the base of Nelson's Column in Trafalgar Square **minus** the number of plagues of Egypt in the Bible **minus** the number of jurors in a criminal trial

Longitude: The number of pounds in a stone **multiplied by** the number of consecutive strikes in tenpin bowling known as a 'turkey' **plus** the number of hills in Rome

CORNELIS GILES

Latitude: The number of circles of hell in Dante's *Inferno* **multiplied by** the number of swans a-swimming in the 'Twelve Days of Christmas' **plus** the number of holes on a golf course

WILLIAM SCORESBY SR.

Latitude: The number of stars in the EU flag **multiplied by** the smallest positive integer that is neither a prime nor a square number **plus** the number of Nazgûl in *The Lord of the Rings*

Longitude: The sum of the first three prime numbers **plus** the number of numbers on a dartsboard

SIR WILLIAM EDWARD PARRY

Latitude: The address number on Pennsylvania Avenue of the White House **divided by** the number of pawns in a chess set **minus** the number of yards away from the goal the edge of the penalty area is situated in soccer

Longitude: The answer to the 'ultimate question of life, the universe and everything' according to Douglas Adams **plus** the number of points awarded for a penalty in rugby union

SIR ALBERT HASTINGS MARKHAM

Latitude: The number of miles in a marathon to the nearest whole number **multiplied by** the number of Noble Truths in Buddhism **minus** the minimum legal age to purchase alcohol in the USA

Longitude: The number of lines in a sonnet **plus** the number of legs insects have

ADOLPHUS GREELY

Latitude: A platinum wedding anniversary in years **plus** the number of the 'Death' card in a Tarot deck

Longitude: The number of syllables in a traditional haiku **plus** the number of books in the *Harry Potter* series

FRIDTJOF NANSEN

Latitude: The number of the Apollo mission that first landed on the Moon **multiplied by** the number of canine teeth in an adult human **plus** the number of Bill Clinton's presidency in the sequence of USA presidents

Longitude: The number of carats representing 100% pure gold **minus** the number a boxing referee counts to in order to declare a winner by knockout

FASCINATING FACT: After the First World War, Nansen became involved with the League of Nations, the forerunner to the United Nations, and helped to repatriate half a million refugees displaced during the conflict. Nansen devised a document for officially stateless citizens to help them cross borders legally, which became known as the Nansen passport (*right*) in his honour. Some of the notable holders included Russian-born author Vladimir Nabokov and composer Igor Stravinsky. In 1922, Nansen was awarded the Nobel Peace Prize for his humanitarian endeavours.

НАНСЕНОВЪ ПАСПОРТЪ

УДОСТОВѢРЕНИЕ ЗА САМОЛИЧНОСТЬ

ВАЖИ ЗА ЕДНА ГОДИНА

24 СТРАНИЦИ   ЦЕНА 175 ЛЕВА

№ 004,810

SEPORT NANSEN

TIFICAT D'IDENTITÉ

VALABLE POUR UN AN

24 PAGES   PRIX 175 LEVAS

GERTRUDE BELL

A LIFE OF 'FIRSTS'

Born in County Durham, England, Gertrude Bell (1868–1926) was a pioneering traveller, explorer, historian, archaeologist and politician. She became the first woman to graduate from Oxford with a first-class degree in Modern History. A woman of means, she spent the next decade travelling the world by steamship, learning languages and developing her skills as an archaeologist, cartographer and mountaineer. She climbed Mont Blanc in 1899 and even had one of the Bernese Alps named in her honour. Over the next 20 years, she travelled extensively through the Arab world, writing multiple books on her experiences.

A fellow of the Royal Geographical Society (RGS), Bell was the first woman to receive the Society's Gill Memorial Award in 1913. The final three years of her life were largely dedicated to creating an archaeological museum in Iraq. Contrary to previous British policy, she advocated that antiquities remain in their country of origin.

FASCINATING FACT: Gertrude Bell met the 22-year-old T. E. Lawrence, later known as Lawrence of Arabia, at the ruins of Carchemish on the Turkey/Syria border in 1911. In 1915, both Bell and Lawrence were assigned to the British Army Intelligence Headquarters in Cairo, and their unparalleled expertise of the area, language and customs were integral to the British war effort. At the Cairo Conference in 1921, both Bell and Lawrence were crucially involved in the creation of the modern state of Iraq and recommending Faisal bin Hussein as king of Iraq.

Can you identify the geographical locations of the places Gertrude Bell describes below on the map on pp.122-123?

TEHRAN: 18th JUNE 1892 (FROM *THE LETTERS OF GERTRUDE BELL*)

'Oh the desert round Teheran [sic]! Miles and miles of it with nothing, nothing; ringed in with bleak bare mountains snow crowned and furrowed with the deep courses of torrents. I never knew what desert was till I came here; it is a very wonderful thing to see; and suddenly in the middle of it all, out of nothing, out of a little cold water, springs up a garden. Such a garden! Trees, fountains, tanks, roses and a house in it, the houses which we heard of in fairy tales when we were little: inlaid with tiny slabs of looking-glass in lovely patterns, blue tiled, carpeted, echoing with the sound of running water and fountains.'

CONSTANTINOPLE (FROM *SAFAR NEMEH, PERSIAN PICTURES* BY GERTRUDE BELL, 1894)

'The whole city is bright with twinkling lamps; the carved platforms round the minarets, which are like the capitals of pillars supporting the great dome of the sky, are hung about with lights, and, slung on wires between them, sentences from the Koran blaze out in tiny lamps against the blackness of the night. ... Towards morning the lamps fade and burn out, but at dusk the city again decks herself in her jewels, and casts a glittering reflection into her many waters.'

VENICE: 14th APRIL 1896 (FROM *THE LETTERS OF GERTRUDE BELL*)

'At 2 Mrs. Green and I started out in a splendid gondola and went nearly to the Lido amidst a crowd of boats. It was very gorgeous for the Municipio appeared in splendid gondolas hung with streamers and emblems and rowed by 8 gondoliers in fancy dresses of different colours. About 3 the Hohenzollern (the German Emperor's yacht) steamed in through the Lido port, a magnificent great white ship with all the sailors dressed in white and standing in lines upon the deck.' (Gertrude describes the arrival of Kaiser Wilhelm II)

BERLIN: 22nd JANUARY 1897 (FROM *THE LETTERS OF GERTRUDE BELL*)

'We drove to the Schloss (City Palace) in the glass coach and were saluted by the guard when we arrived. We felt very swell! The Emperor and Empress were standing on a dais at the end of the room and we walked through a sort of passage made by rows and rows of pages dressed in pink. ... I couldn't look at the Empress much as I was so busy avoiding Aunt Mary's train. She introduced me and then stood aside while I made two curtseys.'

MONT BLANC: 28th AUGUST 1899 (FROM *THE LETTERS OF GERTRUDE BELL*)

'At 1:30 we reached the glacier and all put on our ropes... We had about two hours and a half of awfully difficult rock, very solid fortunately, but perfectly fearful. There were two places which Mathon and Marius literally pulled me up like a parcel. I didn't a bit mind where it was steep up, but round corners where the rope couldn't help me! ... and it was absolutely sheer down. The first half-hour I gave myself up for lost. It didn't seem possible that I could get up all that wall without ever making a slip... We reached the summit at 10:10, the rock being quite easy except one place called the Cheval Rouge. It is a red flat stone, almost perpendicular, some 15 feet high, up which you swarm as best you may with your feet against the Meije, and you sit astride, facing the Meije, on a very pointed crest. I sat there while Marius and Mathon went on and then followed them up an overhanging rock of 20 feet or more. The rope came in most handy! We stayed on the summit until 11. It was gorgeous, quite cloudless... I went to sleep for half-an-hour.'

JERUSALEM: 13th DECEMBER 1899 (FROM *THE LETTERS OF GERTRUDE BELL*)

'One's first impression of Jerusalem is extremely interesting, but certainly not pleasing. The walls are splendid (Saracenic on Jewish foundations), but all the holy places are terribly marred by being built over with hideous churches of all the different sects.'

PETRA: 29th MARCH 1900 (FROM *THE LETTERS OF GERTRUDE BELL*)

'We went on in ecstasies until suddenly between the narrow opening of the rocks, we saw the most beautiful sight I have ever seen. Imagine a temple cut out of the solid rock, the charming facade supported on great Corinthian columns standing clear, soaring upwards to the very top of the cliff in the most exquisite proportions and carved with groups of figures almost as fresh as when the chisel left them all this in the rose red rock, with the sun just touching it and making it look almost transparent.'

DAMASCUS: 11th MAY 1900 (FROM *THE LETTERS OF GERTRUDE BELL*)

'I had a very beautiful ride into Damascus. The air was sweet with the smell of figs and vines and chestnuts, the pomegranates were in the most flaming blossom, the valley was full of mills and mill races bordered by long regiments of poplars – lovely, it must be at all times, but when one comes to it out of the desert it seems a paradise.'

PALMYRA: 20th MAY 1900 (FROM *THE LETTERS OF GERTRUDE BELL*)

'Except Petra, Palmyra is the loveliest thing I have seen in this country. ... It's a fine approach, the hills forming a kind of gigantic avenue with a low range at the end behind which Palmyra stands, and the flat desert, very sandy here, running up to them. ... As we drew near Palmyra, the hills were covered with the strangest buildings, great stone towers, four stories [sic] high, some more ruined and some less, standing together in groups or bordering the road.'

MATTERHORN: 31st AUGUST 1904 (FROM *THE LETTERS OF GERTRUDE BELL*)

'It is very imposing, the Matterhorn... the great faces of rock are so enormous, so perpendicular. ... The most difficult place on the mountain is an overhanging bit above the Tyndall Grat [sic] and quite near the summit. There is usually a rope ladder there, but this year it is broken... There is a fixed rope, which is good and makes descent on this side quite easy, but it is a different matter getting up. We took over 2 hours over this 30 or 40 ft... and I look back to it with great respect. At the overhanging bit you had to throw yourself out on the rope and so hanging catch with your right knee a shelving scrap of rock from which you can just reach the top rung which is all that is left of the ladder. That is how it is done.'

BAGHDAD

(from *Amurath to Amurath*, 1911)

'We rode up to Baghdâd along the edge of the Tigris, and as we went, Fattûḥ, who thought little of ruins except as a divertissement [sic] for the gentry, dilated upon the splendours that we were to witness. Especially was he anxious that I should not fail to see the famous cannon which stands near the arsenal, chained to the ground lest it should fly away.'

BABYLON

(from *Amurath to Amurath*, 1911)

'I left the road, hoping to find a direct path across the plain to that great vestige of ancient splendours, but the deep cutting of a water-course, as dry and dead as Babylon itself, barred the way. My mare climbed to the top of the high bank that edged it and we stood gazing over the site of the city.'

ALEPPO

(from *Amurath to Amurath*, 1911)

'If there be a better gate to Asia than Aleppo, I do not know it. A virile population, a splendid architecture, the quickening sense of a fine Arab tradition have combined to give the town an individuality sharply cut, and more than any other Syrian city she seems instinct with an inherent vitality.'

ALEXANDRIA: 20th NOVEMBER 1913 (FROM *THE LETTERS OF GERTRUDE BELL*)

'Alexandria is not much of a place but it makes me feel as if I were dropping back into the East. Oh my East!'

MARY KINGSLEY

A TRULY INDEPENDENT
WOMAN

Mary Kingsley (1862–1900) was an English traveller and author who journeyed through western and equatorial Africa, becoming the first European to travel through parts of Gabon. She brought back collections of specimens from her travels for the British Museum. She was the niece of writer Charles Kingsley and daughter of doctor George Kingsley, who died in 1892 leaving a book on African culture unfinished, which Mary wanted to complete. Following the death of her mother later the same year, Mary's inheritance enabled her to travel extensively.

She left for West Africa in 1893 and wrote with great humour and insight about her expedition in *Travels in West Africa* (1897), which became an instant bestseller. A return trip to the region culminated in the book *West African Studies* (1899), which met with similar success. Mary volunteered as a nurse following the start of the Second Boer War and died of typhoid in Simon's Town, Cape Town, in 1900.

Can you fill in the blanks to complete Mary's witty passages from *Travels in West Africa*?

1. 'I have never hurt a leopard intentionally; I am habitually kind to animals, and besides I do not think it is ladylike to go _____.'

   A: striking things with a stick   B: shooting things with a gun   C: around throwing sharpened objects

2. 'The leopard crouched, I think to spring on me. I can see its great, beautiful, lambent eyes still, and I seized _____ – and flung it straight at them. It was a noble shot; it burst on the leopard's head like a shell and the leopard went for bush one time.'

   A: an earthen water cooler   B: a leather-clad stool
   C: my trusty umbrella

3. 'It was the beginning of August '93 when I first left England for "the Coast" . . . and a friend hastily sent two newspaper clippings, one entitled "A Week in a Palm-oil Tub," which was supposed to describe the sort of accommodation, companions, and fauna likely to be met with on a steamer going to West Africa; the other from *The Daily Telegraph*, reviewing a French book of "Phrases in common use" in Dahomey. The opening sentence in the latter was, "Help, I am _____.'"

   A: British   B: confused   C: drowning

4. 'Nothing hinders a man, Miss Kingsley, half so much as _____, a friend said to me the other day, after nearly putting his opinion to a practical test.'

A: dying   B: a glass of wine   C: a lack of tea

5. 'It is at these times you realise the blessing of _____. Had I paid heed to the advice of many people in England, who ought to have known better, and did not do it themselves, and adopted masculine garments, I should have been spiked to the bone, and done for.'

A: a corset   B: a good thick skirt
C: a long petticoat

6. 'The way the old chief held it out, and the amount of dollars he asked for it, was enough to make any one believe that I was in such urgent need of the thing, that I was at his mercy regarding price. I waved it off with a haughty scorn, and then feeling smitten by the expression of agonised bewilderment on his face, I dashed him a belt that delighted him, and went inside and _____ to soothe my outraged feelings.'

A: spoke impolitely   B: shut the door firmly
C: had tea

7. 'I receive a most kindly welcome from a fair, grey-eyed German gentleman, only unfortunately I see my efforts to appear before him clean and tidy have been quite unavailing, for he views my appearance with unmixed horror, and suggests _____.
I decline. Men can be trying!'

A: an instant hot bath   B: a hair clip
C: a touch of rouge

Mary Kingsley sitting in a canoe travelling on the Ogowe river.

FRANCIS YOUNGHUSBAND

THE FATHER OF HIMALAYAN EXPLORATION

Francis Younghusband (1863–1942) was a British army officer and explorer. At the age of 23, Younghusband crossed the Gobi Desert and established a route from Kashgar, China to Kashmir through the uncharted Mustagh Pass, earning him election to the Royal Geographical Society as their youngest fellow and a Gold Medal.

Younghusband's name is indelibly linked with the highly controversial British Expedition to Tibet in 1903–1904, which ultimately resulted in the deaths of several hundred Tibetans and the signing of a punitive treaty. However, he experienced a spiritual epiphany while in Tibet, expressing regret for his military actions. He later became instrumental in the formation of the World Congress of Faiths in 1936, which aimed to bring together most of the world's religions to seek common ground.

As President of the RGS, Younghusband formed the Mount Everest Committee, combining the expertise of the Society and The Alpine Club. The Committee coordinated the 1921 Mount Everest Reconnaissance Expedition and the first attempts to scale the mountain in 1922 and 1924. The committee became the Joint Himalayan Committee, which organised Edmund Hillary and Tenzing Norgay's successful ascent of Everest in 1953.

> **FASCINATING FACT:** Younghusband's athletic prowess was legendary in his youth, and he completed the 300-yard dash in 33 seconds – a world record at the time.

Among the first ascents – can you work out which mountain from each continent is missing from the table opposite?

Everest – Asia

Elbrus (west summit) – Europe

Puncak Jaya [Carstensz Pyramid] – Australasia

Denali [Mount McKinley] – North America

Kilimanjaro – Africa

Aconcagua – South America

Vinson – Antarctica

HEIGHT	FIRST CONFIRMED ASCENT	CLIMBERS	MOUNTAIN?
4,884m	February 1962	Heinrich Harrer, Russell Kippax, Albert Huizenga and Philip Temple	
4,892m	December 1966	Barry Corbet, John Evans, William Long, Peter Schoening	
5,642m	Summer 1874	Florence Crauford Grove, Frederick Gardner, Horace Walker, Peter Knubel	
5,895m	October 1889	Hans Meyer and Ludwig Purtscheller	
6,194m	June 1913	Walter Harper, Harry Karstens, Hudson Stuck and Robert Tatum	
6,962m	January 1897	Matthias Zurbriggen	
8,848m	May 1953	Edmund Hillary and Tenzing Norgay	

NELLIE BLY

AROUND THE WORLD IN (LESS THAN) 80 DAYS

Nellie Bly was a pseudonym used by trailblazing American journalist Elizabeth Cochran (1864–1922), who famously circumnavigated the world in an attempt to beat the record of 80 days 'set' by fictional voyager Phileas Fogg in Jules Verne's *Around the World in Eighty Days*. She completed it in 72 days, 6 hours, 11 minutes and 14 seconds.

> **FASCINATING FACT: Nellie Bly took an undercover assignment in 1887, feigning insanity to become admitted to the Women's Lunatic Asylum on Blackwell's Island in New York. The book she wrote about her experience – *Ten Days in a Mad-house* – became a sensational exposé, triggering a grand jury investigation and a significant increase in the Department of Public Charities and Corrections annual budget.**

Can you spot the extraordinary truths amid the tall tales below?

1A Nellie Bly went out of her way to meet Jules Verne in France during her journey and the author wished her good luck.

1B Nellie Bly went out of her way to meet author Robert Louis Stevenson in Italy during her journey and the author wished her good luck.

1C Nellie Bly went out of her way to meet author Bram Stoker in Sri Lanka (Ceylon) during her journey and the author wished her good luck.

2A Nellie Bly invented and secured a patent for a coin-operated newspaper vending machine.

2B Nellie Bly invented and secured a patent for both a new type of milk can and a stacking garbage can.

2C Nellie Bly invented and secured a patent for a mosquito net that fixed around a collar and covered a person's face.

3A While in Brindisi, Nellie rescued an injured Collie dog called McGinty, who accompanied her for the remainder of the journey.

3B While in Ceylon, Nellie bought a sloth bear called McGinty, who accompanied her for the remainder of the journey.

3C While in Singapore, Nellie bought a monkey called McGinty, who accompanied her for the remainder of the journey.

4A Bly's journalistic career began with a furious response to an editorial entitled 'What Girls are Good For' in the *Pittsburgh Dispatch* in 1888 which impressed the editor so much he gave her a job.

4B Bly's journalistic career began with a furious response to an editorial in 1888 about denying universal suffrage which Nellie titled 'Suffragists are Men's Superiors', which impressed the editor so much he gave her a job.

4C Bly's journalistic career began with a furious response to an editorial in 1888 about zoo cruelty which Nellie titled 'Penguins are Snow Joke' which impressed the editor so much he gave her a job.

Put your geographical skills (or the skills of your geography teacher!) to the test on this special 'dotted' map of the world to pinpoint the following 12 places that Nellie stopped at during her round the world voyage.

If you get within two dots of any place, that's an excellent effort. If you get any bang on, give yourself a pat on the back.

San Francisco	Aden
Chicago	Colombo
New York	Penang
Southampton	Singapore
Brindisi	Singapore
Port Said	Hong Kong
	Yokohama

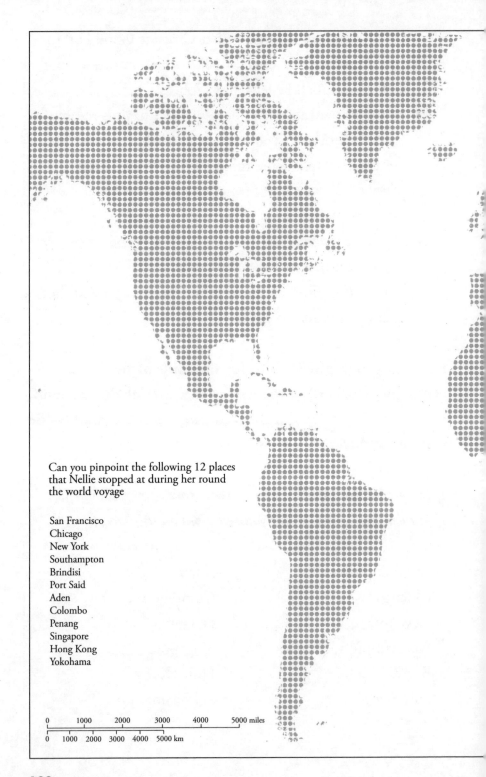

Can you pinpoint the following 12 places
that Nellie stopped at during her round
the world voyage

San Francisco
Chicago
New York
Southampton
Brindisi
Port Said
Aden
Colombo
Penang
Singapore
Hong Kong
Yokohama

0   1000   2000   3000   4000   5000 miles

0   1000 2000 3000 4000 5000 km

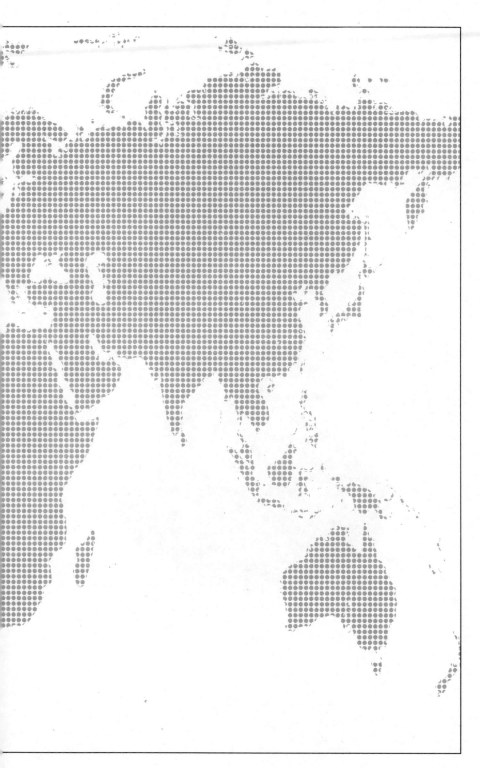

SVEN HEDIN

TRAILBLAZING EXPLORER OF CENTRAL ASIA

Sven Hedin (1865–1952) was a Swedish explorer who undertook four major expeditions to Central Asia and Tibet, mapping previously uncharted areas and visiting important ancient archaeological sites. His ruthless determination did attract criticism, such as his choice to continue through the Taklamakan Desert in April 1895 after realising he had miscalculated the amount of water he, his escorts and camels would need. Towards the end of the trek, Hedin saved the life of one of his companions by going on ahead and returning with water carried in his tall, leather boots.

Nevertheless, Hedin is regarded as a pioneering figure in the history of the exploration of Central Asia and was highly decorated by European monarchs, scientific societies and universities. However, his association with Hitler and Nazi Germany severely damaged his international reputation and his legacy in his later years.

Sven Hedin travelling across Russian Central Asia on a Bactrian camel.

FASCINATING FACT: While traveling through the Lop desert in 1933–1934, Hedin discovered ruins of signal towers which proved that the Great Wall of China once extended as far west as Xinjiang.

Which cities is Sven Hedin describing?

1. 'The desolate landscape was enveloped in a cloud of mist. I dreamt of the tales in the "Arabian Nights", and of all the wealth and splendor that gave the capital of the Abbasid caliphs such fame throughout the Orient. But the haze lifted. I saw only common clay houses and palm trees. The dream vanished. A frail pontoon bridge spanned the Tigris.'

   A: Beirut   B: Casablanca   C: Baghdad

2. 'One of the most beautiful cities in the world, situated as it is on the narrow Bosphorus – which connects two seas and separates two continents – the Golden Horn and the Sea of Marmora.'

A: Constantinople   B: Alexandria   C: Damascus

3. 'After a touching farewell from my family, we boarded a steamer which took us across the Baltic and the Gulf of Finland. From Kronstadt we saw the gilded dome of St. Isaac's, gleaming like the sun; and a few hours later we landed at the Neva Quay in _____.'

A: Moscow   B: St Petersburg   C: Copenhagen

4. 'We approached the Caspian Sea. . . . The engine worked desperately against the opposing head-wind. We puffed and panted heavily along the shore, seeing only indistinctly the white-capped waves as they tossed and broke. The train stopped at last, at _____, the " City of the Winds," which that evening surely deserved its name. The peninsula of Apsheron extends almost fifty miles eastward into the Caspian Sea. _____ is situated on the south coast of this peninsula.'

A: Baku   B: Tehran   C: Kabul

5. 'I knew that a Swedish physician, ranking as a Persian nobleman and bearing the honourable title of Khan, or prince, had been the dentist to the Shah of Persia

since 1873; upon arriving at _____, I drove directly to his house. Happy at meeting a compatriot at last, he received me with open arms, and for a time I lived in his beautiful home, the decorations of which were an approach to Persian style. One day Dr. Hybennet and I were walking between the yellow clay walls and houses of _____'s dusty streets. These streets, where sufficiently wide, had narrow open ditches along their sides, and rows of plane trees, poplars, willows or mulberry trees.

A: Damascus   B: Thebes   C: Tehran

6. 'At noon we glide in between a small holm and the island into the excellent and roomy harbour of _____, well sheltered on all sides from wind and waves. A flotilla of steam launches comes out to meet us as we glide slowly among innumerable vessels to our anchorage and buoys. Here flutter in the wind the flags of all commercial nations; the English, Chinese, Japanese, American, and German colours fly side by side. The water in the harbour basin is so shallow that the turn of the propeller stirs up the greyish-brown mud from the bottom.'

A: Hanoi   B: Hong Kong   C: Bangkok

THE
COLLECTIONS

QUIZ 2

MUNGO PARK

'I SHALL SET SAIL FOR THE EAST
WITH THE FIXED RESOLUTION TO
DISCOVER THE TERMINATION OF THE
NIGER OR PERISH IN THE ATTEMPT'

Mungo Park (1771–1806) was a young Scotsman born to a tenant farmer and his wife. He studied medicine and botany at the University of Edinburgh and was introduced to influential naturalist Sir Joseph Banks in London. On Banks's recommendation, Park was appointed assistant surgeon onboard the East India Company's ship *Worcester*, travelling to Sumatra and returning in 1794.

In 1794, Park became involved in the African Association, an organisation dedicated to exploring West Africa and later subsumed with the Royal Geographical Society. He was asked to discover the mysterious Niger river and its source. Park partly succeeded in his endeavour, observing its flow from west to east, and managed to return safely. He published his experiences in the successful 1799 book *Travels in the Interior Districts of Africa*.

In 1805, he set out to find the source of the river and made it to the Bussa Rapids in modern-day north-western Nigeria. However, the boat became stuck on a rock within arrowshot of indigenous people defending their land. Park and his companions swam into the river to escape them, but drowned.

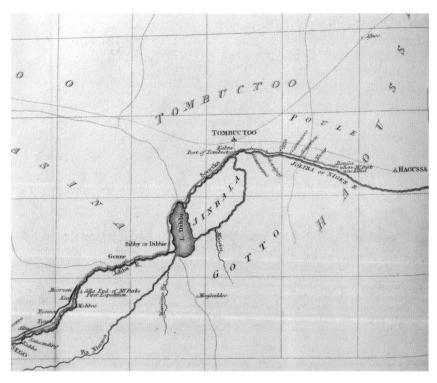

This map is taken from *The Journal of a Mission to the Interior of Africa in the Year 1805*, which was published after Park's death. The map shows the approximate location of Park's demise.

Can you find the following locations on Park's map overleaf of his route to Niger from the description he gives?

1. '...a small village in the king of Yany's dominions, established by British subjects as a factory for trade... It is situated on the banks of the Gambia, sixteen miles above Jonkakonda.'

2. '...and at noon the next day, (December 5th) we reached _____, the capital of the King of Woolli's dominions.'

3. 'At daylight we departed from Karankalla, and as it was but a short day's journey to _____, we travelled slower than usual, and amused ourselves by collecting such eatable fruits as grew near the road-side. About noon we saw at a distance the capital of Kaarta, situated in the middle of an open plain...'

4. 'On his arrival at _____ he got acquainted with certain Moorish merchants who were travelling to Tisheet (a place near the salt pits in the Great Desert, ten days' journey to the northward) to purchase salt.'

5. 'This happened to be a market-day at _____, and the roads were every where filled with people carrying different articles to sell. We passed four large villages, and at eight o'clock saw the smoke over _____. As we approached the town, I was fortunate enough to

overtake the fugitive Kaartans, to whose kindness I had been so much indebted on my journey through Bambarra.'

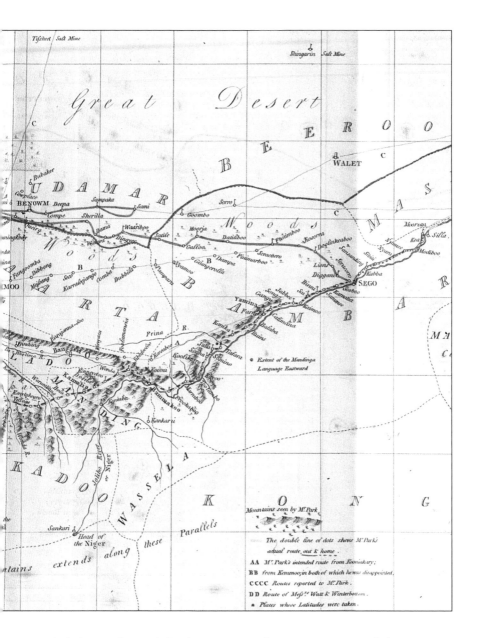

6. 'About four o'clock we arrived at Moorzan, a fishing
   town on the northern bank; from whence I was
   conveyed across the river to _____, a large town;
   where I remained until it was quite dark, under a tree,
   surrounded by hundreds of people.'

FASCINATING FACT: German cartographer Christian Gottlieb Reichard (1758–1837), who never visited Africa and indeed never left Germany, first solved the riddle of the course of the Niger. After considering comparable rivers, he correctly suggested (although his theory was then discredited) that the Niger emptied into the Bight of Benin. It wasn't until 1830, and the travels of English explorers John and Richard Lander, that Reichard's suggestions were proved to be accurate.

Can you solve the anagrams buried among the text from Mungo Park's *Travels in the Interior Districts of Africa?*

1. 'The leaves of the DIG ION when fresh gathered are pounded in a wooden mortar, and mixed in a large earthen jar, with a strong ley of wood ashes; chamber-ley is sometimes added. The cloth is steeped in this mixture, and allowed to remain until it has acquired the proper shade.'

2. 'The few wild animals which inhabit these melancholy regions are the ONE PETAL and the TORCH IS; their swiftness of foot enabling them to reach the distant watering-places.'

3. 'The Gambia abounds with fish, some species of which are excellent food; but none of them that I recollect are known in Europe. At the entrance from the sea sharks are found in great abundance, and,

higher up, GOALS TRAIL and the PATIO MUSH POP are very numerous.'

4. 'No sooner did they conceive themselves safe, than a huge CIDER COOL rose up close to the canoe, plunging near it with much violence: one blow from him would have split it to pieces.'

5. 'I concluded, and was assured by the king's brothers, that no further demands would be made; but was much surprised when our guide and the king's brothers told me on their return that I must send ten bars of GREW POUND and ten of flints.'

6. 'Poultry of all kinds (the turkey excepted) is every where to be had. The WOEFUL GAIN and GRIPED ART/RAT/TAR abound in the fields.'

7. 'After they had gone up about thirty miles, the banks had an appearance of greater consistency, and the beautiful, but deadly VENOM RAG tree was no longer visible.'

CHARLES DARWIN

REVOLUTIONARY NATURALIST

The 22-year-old Charles Darwin (1809–1882) embarked upon HMS *Beagle*'s second surveying voyage to South America as an unpaid naturalist. This five-year-long expedition would change the study of science and natural history forever. Darwin's research and observations helped to formulate his theory of evolution through natural selection and were made famous through the publication of *On the Origin of Species*, 20 years later.

'The voyage of the *Beagle* has been by far the most important event in my life, and has determined my whole career. Everything about which I thought or read was made to bear directly on what I had seen or was likely to see; and this habit of mind was continued during the five years of the voyage. I feel sure that it was this training which has enabled me to do whatever I have done in science.'

The Life and Letters of Charles Darwin, 1887

See if you can win Darwin's seal of approval by answering these brainteasers

1. Arriving at Tenerife, the crew of the *Beagle* were told that they had to remain on board for a 12-day quarantine period because of a recent outbreak of which contagious disease in England?

2. What is the name of the island off the east coast of Africa that Darwin refers to by its historic name the 'Isle of France'?

3. What occurred on 20 February 1835, while Darwin was in Chile, that destroyed the city of Concepción?

4. The *Beagle* contained a library of around 400 books but Darwin's reading was not always scientific. He often carried around a well-worn copy of which 17th-century epic poem?

5. What weather phenomenon did Darwin witness in the estuary of the Rio de la Plata near Montevideo, Uruguay, that he described as 'nature's fireworks'?

6. 'It does ones [sic] heart good to hear how things are going on in England – Hurrah for the honest Whigs – I trust they will soon attack that monstrous stain on our boasted liberty…' What is Darwin referring to in a letter to a friend on 2 June 1833?

7. Which nightmarish blood-sucking creature wrought havoc among the horses Darwin's party rode through Brazil?

Can you guess the animal that is being described?

1. 'They were diving and playing about the surface of the water, but showed so little of their bodies, that they might easily have been mistaken for water-rats. Mr. Browne shot one: certainly it is a most extraordinary animal; a stuffed specimen does not at all give a good idea of the appearance of the head and beak when fresh; the latter becoming hard and contracted.'

    A: Sea Otter   B: Duck-billed Platypus
    C: Giant Cuttlefish

2. '… each of which must have weighed at least two hundred pounds: one was eating a piece of cactus, and as I approached, it stared at me and slowly walked away; the other gave a deep hiss, and drew in its head.'

    A: Giant Tortoise   B: Komodo Dragon
    C: Giant Anteater

3. 'It is a hideous-looking creature, of a dirty black colour, stupid, and sluggish in its movements… Their tails are flattened sideways, and all four feet partially webbed. They are occasionally seen some hundred yards from the

shore, swimming about; and Captain Collnett, in his *Voyage* says, "They go to sea in herds a-fishing, and sun themselves on the rocks; and may be called alligators in miniature".'

A: Common Snapping Turtle   B: Marine Iguana
C: Black-spotted Newt

Above: Charles Darwin's pocket sextant, carried on the voyage of His Majesty's Ship Beagle 1831-1836, stored in a brass case. This was presented to the RGS by Charles Darwin's son, Leonard, in 1912.

4. 'Nature, in these climes, chooses her vocalists from more humble performers than in Europe. A small _____, of the genus Hyla, sits on a blade of grass about an inch above the surface of the water, and sends forth a pleasing chirp: when several are together they sing in harmony on different notes.'

A: Cricket   B: Frog   C: Beetle

DARWIN'S FINCHES

'Darwin's finches' are a group of around 15 species of birds collected on the Galápagos Islands by Darwin during the second voyage of HMS *Beagle*.

Darwin realised that these birds possess different beak shapes from similar birds on the mainland. Because these birds have spent generations on the islands, isolated from the mainland, their beaks have adapted to the food they eat. This kind of adaptation shows natural selection in action as a key mechanism of evolution.

> **TRIVIA: Confusingly, 'Darwin's finches' are not actually finches, but belong to the tanager family. Also, the term 'Darwin's finches' was never used by him; it was first employed by English ornithologist and surgeon Percy Lowe in 1936.**

An illustration of a pair of Common cactus finches from the 1841 volume on birds ('Part III: Birds') that forms part of the multi-volume work *The Zoology of the Voyage of HMS Beagle*, edited and superintended by Charles Darwin.

Sven Hedin at the University of Paris, France.

KATHERINE ROUTLEDGE

AMONG THE STONE GIANTS

Katherine Routledge (1866–1935) was an archaeologist and anthropologist who, along with her husband William Scoresby Routledge, famously undertook the first scientific survey of the *moai* (ancient monoliths) on Easter Island in 1914. Katherine published her findings in the popular travel book *The Mystery of Easter Island* in 1919. She had begun the first of her overseas travels in 1902, travelling to South Africa to investigate the resettlement of single working women from England there.

Sadly, Katherine is believed to have suffered from paranoid schizophrenia. Her mental health deteriorated and she was committed to a secure asylum in Sussex where she died in 1935.

THE MOAI

(Easter Island monoliths)

Many *moai* have been removed from Easter Island, an overseas territory of Chile. Three of the remarkable monoliths are housed in cities around Chile, while several others are controversially displayed in museums around the world. Others are in private hands. The most famous *moai* held abroad is Hoa Hakananai'a, one of the most spiritually significant of the ancient monoliths, which was taken by the crew of HMS *Topaze* in 1868 as a gift for Queen Victoria.

Can you work out the location of these *moai* around the world from the clues?

1. Home to the world's oldest underground railway system, which opened in January 1863

2. American city that contains the largest library in the world

3. The Roman city of Lutetia was the predecessor to this famous European city

4. The headquarters of NATO and the European Commission

5. The second-largest city on New Zealand's South Island. The city's name comes from the Scottish Gaelic name for Edinburgh

MATTHEW HENSON

UNSUNG HERO OF
THE ARCTIC

Matthew Henson (1866–1955) was an African-American explorer who played a vital role in Robert Peary's expeditions to the Arctic, including the 1908–1909 expedition to the North Pole.

Many regard Henson as the de facto leader of Peary's North Pole expedition, with his ability to hunt, drive and fix the sledges, look after the men and other dogs, and speak the Inuit languages. On 6th April 1909, Henson and Pearcy arrived at what they believed was the North Pole. Henson later wrote, 'As I stood there at the top of the world and thought of the hundreds of men who had lost their lives in the effort to reach it, I felt profoundly grateful that I had the honour of representing my race in the historic achievement.' Despite a rival claim by explorer Frederick A. Cook to have reached the Pole the previous year, the National Geographic Society credited Peary with the distinction. Henson had to wait until 1944 until he was awarded the Congressional Medal that had been awarded to all of the other members of the Peary expedition.

FASCINATING FACT: On 6th April 1988, Matthew Henson's body was moved from Woodlawn Cemetery in New York and reinterred at Arlington National Cemetery in Washington, D.C., next to the tomb of Robert Peary.

Matthew Henson (in the centre), surrounded by four Inuit guides, at what they believed was the North Pole.

Matthew Henson was posthumously awarded the coveted Hubbard Medal by the National Geographic Society in 2000. The first recipient of the medal in 1906 was Robert Peary. Can you name the selected others from the clues below?

1907: Norwegian explorer who became the first to reach the South Pole

1910: Heroic leader of the 1914 *Endurance* expedition

1927: Aviator who famously crossed the Atlantic solo in the *Spirit of St. Louis*

1969: Command module pilot of *Apollo 8*, the first Apollo mission to enter lunar orbit, and later commander of the ill-fated *Apollo 13* mission

1970: All three members of the historic *Apollo 11* mission

1995: The world's foremost expert on chimpanzees, who founded a famous institute that bears her name

2013: Writer and Director of *Avatar*, who famously reached the Challenger Deep solo in 2012

ROBERT FALCON SCOTT

TRAGIC HERO OF THE ANTARCTIC

Robert Falcon Scott (1868–1912) was a Royal Naval officer and explorer who led two Antarctic expeditions. On the second of these he reached the South Pole on the 17th January 1912. Unfortunately, his rival, Roald Amundsen, had reached the Pole several weeks earlier. On the return journey Scott and his four companions all died before they could reach a supply depot.

Scott's first expedition – the National Antarctic Expedition – was masterminded by RGS President, Sir Clements Markham. This expedition lasted from 1901–1904 and included an extensive programme of scientific research. In 1902 Scott, Edward Wilson and Ernest Shackleton made a round-trip sledge journey of 960 miles reaching a new farthest south record at 82° 17' south. Scott also made the first balloon ascent in the Antarctic.

From the following list, can you add the names of the lead vessels of each expedition to the table below? On the map plot the positions of the holders of the farthest south record. We've plotted Cook's farthest south record from 1774 on the map to help you out.

Fram

Nimrod

Jane

Erebus

Resolution

Erebus

Discovery

Southern Cross

EXPLORER	DATE	POSITION	NAME OF LEAD VESSEL
A. James Cook	30th January 1774	71°10'S, 130°W	
B. James Weddell	20th February 1823	74°15'S, 30°12'W	
C. James Clark Ross	8th February 1841	78°S, 164°W	
D. James Clark Ross	23rd January 1842	78°10'S, 164°W	
E. Carsten Borchgrevink	16th February 1900	78°50'S, 162°W	
F. Robert Falcon Scott	30th December 1902	82°17'S, 165°E	
G. Ernest Shackleton	9th January 1909	88°23'S, 162°E	
H. Roald Amundsen	14th December 1911	90°	

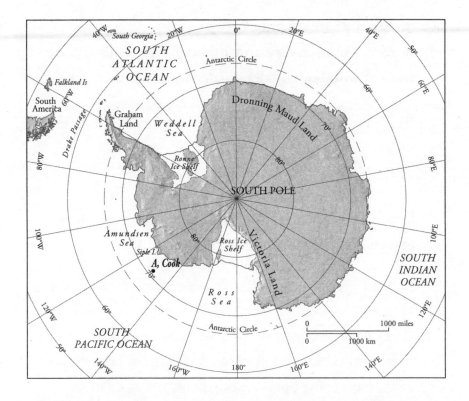

FASCINATING FACT: Among the rocks collected by Scott and discovered on his sledge, scientists found a fossil sample of a Glossopteris fern – the first Antarctic fossil ever discovered. Fossils of this fern had already been found in Australia, South America and India, providing crucial support to the theory that many continents were once linked together in one vast supercontinent.

Can you work out which Antarctic creature Scott is describing?

1. '. . . unappeasably voracious, devouring or attempting to devour every smaller animal . . . instances have

occurred where a band of _____ laid siege to whales in tow, and although frequently lanced and cut with boat spades, made away with their prey.'

A: Leopard Seal   B: Killer Whale   C: Sperm Whale

2. '. . . one occasionally sees the long lithe _____, formidably armed with ferocious teeth and doubtless containing a penguin or two and perhaps a young crab-eating seal.'

A: Sea Leopard   B: Killer Whale   C: Elephant Seal

3. 'They have lost none of their attractiveness, and are most comical and interesting; as curious as ever, they will always come up at a trot when we sing to them.'

A: Weddell Seal   B: Black-browed Albatross
C: Adélie Penguin

4. 'One sees first a small dark hump appear and then immediately a jet of grey fog squirted upwards fifteen to eighteen feet, gradually spreading as it rises vertically into the frosty air. I have been nearly in these blows once or twice and had the moisture in my face with a sickening smell of shrimpy oil. Then the bump elongates and up rolls an immense blue-grey or blackish grey round back with a faint ridge along the top, on which presently appears a small hook-like dorsal fin, and then the whole sinks and disappears.'

A: Humpback Whale   B: Blue Whale
C: Sperm Whale

5. 'All other birds fled north when the severity of winter
descended upon us: the _____
alone was prepared to face the extremest rigors of
our climate; and we gathered no small satisfaction
from being the first to throw light on the habits of a
creature, which so far surpasses in hardihood all others
of the feathered tribe.'*

A: Black-browed Albatross   B: Antarctic Tern
C: Emperor Penguin

6. 'Necessarily progress became slow, but life abounds
in the pack, and the birds that came to visit the ship
were a source of perpetual interest. The pleasantest
and most constant of these visitors was the small
_____, with its dainty snow-white
plumage relieved only by black beak and feet, and
black, beady eye.'*

A: Snowy Sheathbill   B: Snow Petrel
C: Snowy Owl

* From *The Voyages Of Captain Scott* Retold from *The Voyage of
the 'Discovery'* and *Scott's Last Expedition* by Charles Turley

ROALD AMUNDSEN

PIONEERING POLAR
EXPLORER

Roald Amundsen (1872–1928) was a Norwegian polar explorer who became the first person to reach the South Pole on 14th December 1911. He was also the first explorer to navigate the Northwest Passage – the seaway across the Arctic that links the Atlantic and Pacific Oceans – by ship, on a voyage that lasted from 1903 to 1906.

Amundsen went missing, presumed dead, on 18th June 1928 aboard a seaplane while undertaking a rescue mission to find the survivors of the *Italia* airship, which had crashed in the Arctic. In all, 17 crew and rescuers perished.

> **FASCINATING FACT:** When Amundsen departed Oslo, Norway on 3rd June 1910, only his brother knew that Amundsen intended to reach the South Pole rather than the North, which had been his original intention. In October 1910, while in Australia, Scott received a telegram from Amundsen that read: 'Beg to inform you Fram proceeding Antarctic – Amundsen.'

Can you match the correct number to the fact?

4,500	3,200
19	1,860
11	99
7	52
56	39
34	

A The number of Greenland sledge dogs Amundsen took in October 1911

B The number of minus degrees Celsius that Amundsen had to contend with on his first attempt for the Pole in September 1911

C The number of dogs that survived the expedition

D The number of days to travel to the Pole and back from Framheim, the team's Antarctic base

E The distance in nautical miles they had covered

F Amundsen's age when he reached the South Pole

G The number of days Amundsen beat Scott to the Pole by

H Total number of crew members on the *Fram*

I The summit in metres of the Axel Heiberg Glacier

J The number of calories allocated per person per day

K The number of depots Amundsen had constructed along the way

Can you find the fiction about the South Pole buried among the extraordinary truths?

The sun only rises and sets once a year at the South Pole

Buzz Aldrin is the oldest person to have visited the South Pole

The South Pole sits on a 2,700m-thick sheet of ice

The last aircraft to the permanently manned Amundsen-Scott Research Station leaves in mid-February; the next one returns in late October

The tent that Amundsen erected at the Pole in December 1911 now lies at a depth of 17m below the surface

After Amundsen and Scott, the first person to reach the South Pole overland was Edmund Hillary

On 3rd August 1958, the USS *Nautilus* completed the first submerged transit of the South Pole

Chess games were banned at Russian Antarctic stations after two scientists fought over a game in 1959, with the loser attacking the winner with an ice axe

The most southerly marathon takes place at a latitude of 80°S at the foot of the Ellsworth Mountains

Measurements from the Halley Research Station in Antarctica led to the discovery of the ozone hole in 1985

Match the route to the explorer in the map

A. Sir John Franklin's lost expedition attempting to navigate the Northwest Passage (1845–1847)

B. Nils Adolf Erik Nordenskiöld's successful Northeast Passage expedition (1878–1879)

C. Fridtjof Nansen sets the farthest north record (1895)

D. Roald Amundsen successfully navigates the Northwest Passage (1903–1906)

E. Robert Peary and Matthew Henson claimed to have reached the North Pole (1909)

F. Amundsen reaches the North Pole (1926)

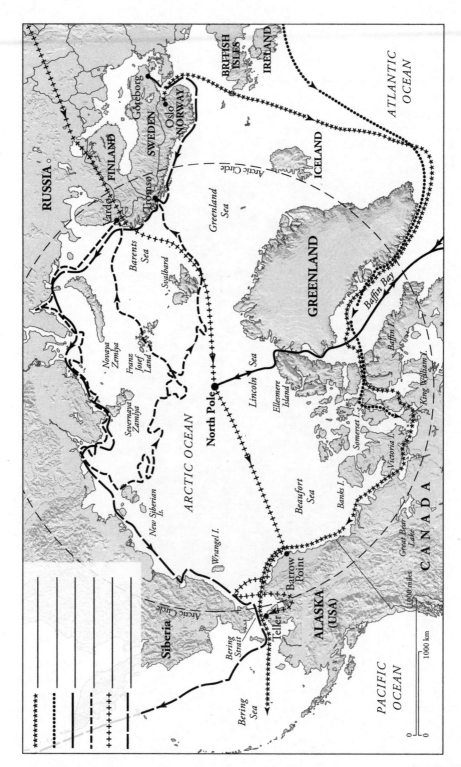

ATLANTIC
OCEAN

BRITISH ISLES

IRELAND

RUSSIA

Göteborg

FINLAND

SWEDEN

Oslo
NORWAY

Tromsø

Vardø

ICELAND

Arctic Circle

Greenland
Sea

Barents
Sea

Svalbard

GREENLAND

Baffin Bay

Novaya
Zemlya

Franz
Josef
Land

Baffin I.

King William I.

Severnaya
Zemlya

North Pole

Lincoln
Sea

Ellesmere
Island

Somerset
I.

Victoria I.

CANADA

New Siberian
Is.

ARCTIC OCEAN

Banks I.

Great Bear
Lake

Wrangel I.

Beaufort
Sea

1000 miles

Barrow
Point

Siberia

Arctic Circle

Teller

ALASKA
(USA)

1000 km

Bering
Strait

Bering
Sea

PACIFIC
OCEAN

0

0

ERNEST SHACKLETON

AN EPIC FEAT OF ENDURANCE

Ernest Shackleton (1874–1922) was an inspirational Anglo-Irish explorer of the Antarctic. He was appointed third lieutenant on Robert Falcon Scott's *Discovery* expedition of 1901–1904 before undertaking three of his own Antarctic expeditions. He attempted to reach the South Pole during the *Nimrod* (1907–1909) expedition – coming within 97 miles of it; strove to cross the Antarctic continent in the *Endurance* (1914–1917) expedition; and the *Quest* expedition, his last Antarctic exploration in 1921–1922.

After the *Endurance* had been crushed by sea ice, Shackleton and five crew members battled extreme hardship to sail one of the ship's lifeboats, the *James Caird*, 800 miles to South Georgia to find help, leaving 22 crew members on Elephant Island. Successfully traversing South Georgia's mountainous interior on foot, the first time this had ever been achieved, he reached the whaling station of Stromness. Three months later, he mounted a rescue mission, saving all of his stranded crew mates.

You've found a message, encrypted using a number of different code systems, which you believe reveals the last-known location of the *Endurance*. You'll have to crack them all to find the coordinates and pinpoint the position on the map.

'• _• _•• ••_ •_• •_ _• _•_• •

••• •• _• _•_ •• _• __•

IXPQ MLPFQFLK

1000101 101

••• ___ ••_ _ ••••

110011 11110

•__ • ••• _

PEXZHIBQLK, LZQLYBO QTBKQV-PBSBKQE, KFKBQBBK CFCQBBK'

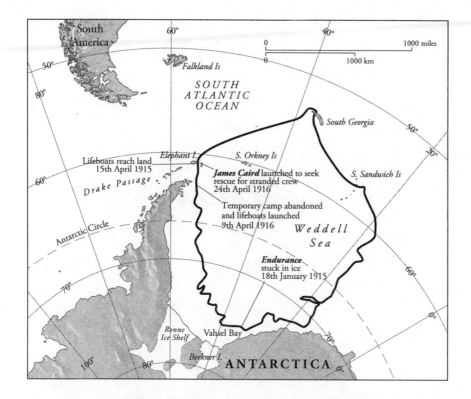

Once you've found out the location, mark the position on the map above. The black line shows the entire *Endurance* expedition.

170

HOWARD CARTER

LEGENDARY EGYPTOLOGIST

Howard Carter (1874–1939) was a British archaeologist, whose discovery of the tomb of Egyptian pharaoh Tutankhamun in 1922 was one of the most significant contributions to the subject of Egyptology.

Carter had begun his archaeological work aged 17, working as an artist at the site of Queen Hatshepsut's temple in Thebes. In 1907, he was introduced to Lord Carnarvon, an antiquities collector, who became Carter's financial backer. In 1915, Carnarvon hired Carter to begin work in the Valley of the Kings – the area containing burial sites of pharaohs and other influential figures in ancient Egypt. By 1922, Carter had little to show for his endeavours and Carnarvon gave him one more season to make a significant find. Then, on 4th November 1922, Carter's team uncovered a staircase that led to the burial site of the Egyptian 'boy pharaoh', Tutankhamun, and one of the most extraordinary discoveries in archaeological history.

The opening of the tomb captured the public imagination and gave rise to many tall tales. Which one of the following is fiction?

Within six weeks of the opening of the tomb, Lord Carnarvon suffered a mosquito bite, which became infected after he nicked it with a razor and he died of blood poisoning.

After hearing the news about Carnarvon's death in April 1923, the superstitious Italian dictator Benito Mussolini ordered the removal of the Egyptian mummy he had received as a gift from a Middle Eastern diplomat earlier that year.

Tutankhamun's mummy was placed within three golden coffins inside a stone sarcophagus, but the feet on the outer coffin were too large and had to be cut away; Carter found the fragments in the base of the sarcophagus.

Sir Arthur Conan Doyle, creator of Sherlock Holmes, suggested to the Press that 'an evil elemental' may have caused Lord Carnarvon's death, whipping up speculation that the tomb was cursed.

Of the 58 people who were present at the opening of Tutankhamun's tomb, a remarkable 50 had died within 12 years.

Among the artefacts in Tutankhamun's tomb were 130 staffs and walking sticks. CT scans revealed that he had been crippled by bone necrosis, which would have necessitated the use of a stick.

We can't exactly match hieroglyphics to the English
alphabet, but we've done our best to fill in the gaps and
create a version for this puzzle. Can you guess the code and
translate the telegram Howard Carter sent to his backer
after unearthing the entrance to the tomb?

TO:

FROM:

HARRIET CHALMERS ADAMS

A FEARLESS PIONEER

Harriet Chalmers Adams (1875–1937) was an American explorer, geographer, photographer and writer. Her first major expedition, starting in 1904, was a three-year journey around all of the constituent countries of South America. Among her achievements, she traversed the Andes on horseback, became the first woman to travel from the Amazon to French Guiana, and retraced the trail of Columbus and the conquistadors. She wrote and provided photographs for a total of 21 articles for *National Geographic Magazine* detailing her extensive travels, and was lauded as a captivating after-dinner speaker.

In 1913, Harriet became one of the first American women members of the Royal Geographical Society. In 1925, she also became the first President of the Society of Women Geographers, which was set up after women were continually denied entry to explorers' clubs.

FASCINATING FACT: In 1916, Harriet became the first woman to be permitted to visit the French front lines as a war correspondent, and one of the only people allowed by the French government to photograph combat.

The following is the title of an article published in the *New York Times* on 18th August 1912, but which part of the headline have we creatively added?

'WOMAN EXPLORER'S HAZARDOUS TRIP IN SOUTH AMERICA; Harriet Chalmers Adams Tells of Encountering Vampires, Shooting Monkeys, Sneaking Past Jaguars, Creeping Along Dangerous Trails–Found a River of Peat–Englishman Immured in a Canyon, Too Fat to Get Out.'

From the clues, can you work out the identity of these extraordinary women who joined the Society of Women Geographers?

1. First female aviator to fly solo across the Atlantic.

2. Former First Lady who served as the first chair of the UN Commission on Human Rights and played a key part in the creation of the UN Declaration of Human Rights.

3. Famously spent nearly 60 years studying wild chimpanzees since first visiting Gombe Stream National Park in Tanzania in 1960.

4. The first American woman to walk in space in October 1984 and part of the team that launched the Hubble Space Telescope.

5. American marine biologist and legendary under-sea explorer described as the 'Queen of the Deep'.

> **FASCINATING FACT:** While travelling across Haiti on horseback, Harriet captured five solenodons – venomous rat-like mammals with elongated snouts thought to be a rare antecedent of the rodent family. Harriet presented three of them to the Bronx Park Zoo in New York and two to the Zoological Gardens in Washington, D.C.

AMELIA EARHART

INSPIRATIONAL AVIATOR

Amelia Earhart (1897–1937) was an American aviation pioneer who became the first woman to fly solo across the Atlantic Ocean. Among her other achievements, she broke several aviation speed records, held the female altitude record and helped form the Ninety-Nines, an international organisation of female pilots. Earhart famously went missing on 2nd July 1937 attempting to circumnavigate the globe in a Lockheed Model 10-E Electra, and her disappearance has been the source of intense speculation to this day.

Three female aviators have been honoured on commemorative USA stamps: Amelia Earhart, Harriet Quimby (1875–1912), who became the first woman to fly solo across the English Channel, and Bessie Coleman (1892–1926), the first woman of Native American and African-American descent to gain a pilot's licence, later becoming a successful air show pilot.

From the clues below, can you name the other famous women whose achievements have been commemorated by the USA postal service?

1. The Powhatan princess who saved the life of Captain John Smith

2. Influential Mexican artist most famous for her autobiographical work

3. Four-time Best Actress winner at the Academy Awards

4. Author of *The Bell Jar*

5. Activist who played a pivotal role in the Montgomery bus boycott

6. Legendary French vocalist of the 1940s

BRAINTEASER: Which hot beverage did Amelia famously enjoy during her first solo flight from Hawaii to California?

RECORD BREAKER

On 20th May 1932, Amelia Earhart piloted a single-engine Lockheed Vega 5B across the Atlantic by herself, battling mechanical problems and unfavourable weather along the way. The flight lasted a record 14 hours and 56 minutes, and earned her the Distinguished Flying Cross (DFC) from the US Congress and the Legion of Honour from the French government. It also cemented her legacy as an aviation legend, and established her as an international celebrity. She returned to the USA on 20th June to a ticker-tape parade in New York City.

1. Amelia Earhart was the second person to fly solo across the Atlantic Ocean. Who was the first?

A: Howard Hawks

B: Charles Lindbergh

C: Jimmy Doolittle

D: Eddie Rickenbacker

2. Amelia Earhart became a nurse's aide treating wounded soldiers, on their return from service, during the first World War. The following year, she helped treat victims of which pandemic?

A: Typhoid

B: Rabies

C: Spanish Flu

D: Polio

3. After successfully making it across the Atlantic solo on 20th May 1932, Amelia landed in a pasture in which country?

A: England

B: Ireland

C: Scotland

D: Northern Ireland

4. In 2013, another female aviator named Amelia Earhart recreated her namesake's 1937 circumnavigation. True or false?

5. Which First Lady did Amelia Earhart befriend and fly with from Baltimore to Washington D.C. in 1933?

A: Grace Coolidge

B: Bess Truman

C: Eleanor Roosevelt

D: Lou Hoover

6. Which of the following jobs did Amelia Earhart not do?

A: Librarian

B: Railway clerk

C: Social worker

D: Telephone operator

> **FASCINATING FACT:** In 1991, a fragment of an aluminium patch was discovered on the remote island of Nikumaroro in the western Pacific. In February 2019, The International Group for Historic Aircraft Recovery (TIGHAR) acquired a 16mm film showing Earhart's plane embarking on a test flight on 1st July 1937. It shows an aluminium patch used to repair the plane's fuselage in Miami. The film is currently being scanned at high-resolution to determine if the recovered aluminium belongs to Earhart's plane.

LOST AT SEA

The table on pp.184-5 shows the 30 legs of Amelia Earhart's flight west to east from Oakland, California to Lae, Papua New Guinea. On 2nd July, she was due to fly from Lae to Howland Island, a tiny atoll in the western Pacific designated as a refuelling stop. At 2,556 miles, it was to be the longest leg of the journey, an ordeal compounded by concerns locating the island. Tragically, despite the presence of the *Itasca*, a US Coast Guard vessel stationed to provide navigational support and radio links, Earhart and her navigator Fred Noonan never reached the island. On 19th July 1937, after an extensive search costing $4 million, they were declared lost at sea.

The list of destinations Earhart flew to has been jumbled except for the entries in bold. Can you rearrange them to find the correct route she took?

(NOTE: the miles column is in the correct order and the entries in bold have been filled in to assist you)

FROM	MILES
Oakland, California, USA	*325*
Fortaleza, Brazil	450
Massawa, Ethiopia (then Italian Eritrea)	1,250
Caripito, Venezuela	675
Port Darwin, Australia	1,033
Bangkok, Thailand (then Siam)	750
Ndjamena, Chad (then French Equatorial Africa)	667
Karachi, Pakistan (then India)	1,200
Burbank, California, USA	268
Natal, Brazil	1,961
Gao, Mali (then French West Africa)	103
Calcutta, India	1,130
El Fasher, Sudan	989
San Juan, Puerto Rico	700
Miami, Florida, USA	501
Dakar, Senegal (then French West Africa)	450
Sittwe, Myanmar (then Burma)	300
Rangoon, Myanmar (then Burma)	1,600
Koepang, Timor, Indonesia	1,390
Singapore, Malaysia	335
Khartoum, Sudan	306
Tucson, Arizona, USA	300

FROM	MILES
Assab, Ethiopia (then Italian Eritrea)	904
New Orleans, Louisiana, USA	560
Bandoeng, Java, Indonesia (then Dutch East Indies)	*355*
Soerabaja, Java, Indonesia (then Dutch East Indies)	*355*
Bandoeng, Java, Indonesia (then Dutch East Indies)	*1,165*
Paramaribo, Suriname (then Dutch Guiana)	500
Saint-Louis, Senegal (then French West Africa)	1,207
Lae, Papua New Guinea (then Territory of New Guinea)	*2,556*
Howland Island	*n/a*

1: Oakland, California, USA

2: _____

3: _____

4: _____

5: _____

6: _____

7: _____

8: _____

9: _____

10: _____

11: _____

12: _____

13: _____

14: _____

15: _____

16: _____

17: _____

18: _____

19: _____

20: _____

21: _____

22: _____

23: _____

24: _____

25: Bandoeng, Java, Indonesia (then Dutch East Indies)

26: Soerdoja, Java, Indonesia

27: Bandoeng, Java, Indonesia

28: _____

29: _____

30: Lae, Papua New Guinea (then Territory of New Guinea)

31: Howland Island

EDMUND HILLARY AND TENZING NORGAY

CONQUERORS OF EVEREST

The 1953 British Mount Everest Expedition was the first successful ascent of the mountain. Led by John Hunt, two pairs of climbers were selected to attempt the summit. The first pair, Tom Bourdillon and Charles Evans, were forced to turn back when Evans's, oxygen set malfunctioned. Three days later, on 29th May, at 11:30am, Edmund Hillary (1919–2008) and Tenzing Norgay (1914–1986) reached the summit. The pair spent about 15 minutes at the top of the world, with Hillary taking photographs, including one of Norgay holding his ice axe. Hillary placed a small cross in the snow and Norgay, a devout Buddhist, buried a small offering of food.

Hillary was a mountaineer and explorer from New Zealand, and Norgay was a Nepalese Sherpa mountaineer who had worked as a high-altitude porter on previous attempts to reach the summit. *The Times* correspondent Jan Morris received the news of their successful ascent the following day and dispatched a runner to the town of Namche Bazaar to forward a coded message to Kathmandu. The news was released in London on 2nd June on the morning of Queen Elizabeth II's coronation.

Hillary and Norgay approach their final camp, at almost 8,354m.

See how you do on our Everest trivia quiz:

1. Everest is known by the name 'Sagarmatha' in Nepali, but what does the word translate to?

A: 'Forehead in the sky'   B: 'The eagle's meeting place'
C: 'The head that wears the crown of snow'

2. Everest is known in Tibetan as 'Chomolungma', but what does this word translate to?

A: 'God the father of the world'   B: 'Goddess mother of mountains'   C: 'Princess of the heavens'

3. What was Everest referred to before it was given its official name by Andrew Waugh, the British Surveyor General of India?

   A: Hill 21   B: Mountain A   C: Peak XV

4. On 23rd May 2013, Yüichirö Miura became the oldest person to climb to the summit of Mount Everest, but how old was he?

   A: 60   B: 70   C: 80

5. The youngest person to reach the top was Jordan Romero in 2010, but how old was he?

   A: 13   B: 15   C: 17

6. Approximately how many calories do mountaineers burn on the day of the summit climb?

   A: 10,000   B: 15,000   C: 20,000

7. How many times had Tenzing Norgay fail to reach the summit before he conquered it in 1953?

   A: 3   B: 6   C: 10

8. Mount Everest and K2 are the two highest mountains in the world, but what is the third highest?

   A: Lhotse   B: Annapurna 1   C: Kangchenjunga

> **FASCINATING FACT:** Everest is the world's highest mountain if measured from sea level, but if measured from the base at which it sits, Hawaii's Mauna Kea, which sits at the bottom of the Pacific Ocean, is an extraordinary 10,200m.

Fact or fiction? Can you spot the two untruths among these extraordinary facts?

In 1952, Tenzing Norgay (along with Swiss mountaineer Raymond Lambert) set the highest altitude record, coming up just 200m short of the south summit of Everest.

Edmund Hillary was the only living person other than a head of state to appear on a New Zealand banknote.

Tenzing Norgay saved Hillary's life shortly before they began their historic climb after Hillary fell into a crevasse and was saved by Norgay swiftly securing the rope using his ice axe.

For their achievements, Edmund Hillary, Tenzing Norgay and John Hunt were all knighted by Queen Elizabeth II.

Norgay broke the record for the deepest dive without swimming aids in 1959, achieving a depth of 100m below sea level off the coast of the Bahamas.

In 1960, Hillary led a scientific expedition to Nepal to try to find the Abominable Snowman.

Hillary was appointed New Zealand's High Commissioner in India and Bangladesh and Ambassador to Nepal from 1985 to 1988.

In 1985, Hillary and Neil Armstrong flew to the North Pole together, but the champagne bottle they brought with them to celebrate their journey froze solid.

In May 2002, Hillary's son Peter climbed Everest. Norgay's son Jamling Tenzing Norgay was also a member of the expedition.

In 2003, honorary citizenship was conferred on Hillary by the government of Nepal – it was the first time that they had awarded such an honour.

NEIL ARMSTRONG

FIRST MAN ON THE MOON

Neil Armstrong (1930–2012) was the first man to set foot on the surface of the Moon, making his 'giant leap for mankind' during the 1969 *Apollo 11* landing. Armstrong became a fighter pilot during the Korean War, and later worked as an experimental research test pilot before becoming an employee at NASA following its establishment in 1958.

In 1966, Armstrong commanded *Gemini 8*, during which he achieved the first docking of two craft in space. Just three years later, he commanded the *Apollo 11* mission, which took off on 16th July 1969. Propelled by the *Saturn V* rocket, with the command vessel *Columbia* attached, they successfully entered orbit. Armstrong and lunar module pilot Buzz Aldrin boarded the *Eagle* landing craft that touched down on the Moon's surface on 20th July. Their journey was broadcast to a television audience of approximately 650 million around the world.

FASCINATING FACT: When Armstrong and Aldrin returned from their moon walk, they found that one of them had accidentally snapped off the switch of a circuit breaker. Realising they could not take off without it, Aldrin improvised, pushing a plastic felt-tip pen into the hole. Thankfully, it worked. Aldrin had only brought along the felt-tip pen because he did not like the zero gravity pens NASA had spent a fortune producing.

Put your lunar knowledge to the test in this quiz:

1. Which of the following is not a sea on the Moon?

   A: Sea of Harmony   B: Sea of Tranquility
   C: Sea of Serenity

2. Which of the following is not a lunar crater?

   A: Kepler Crater   B: Copernicus Crater
   C: Socrates Crater

3. What was the designated number of the final Apollo mission to go ahead?

   A: 15   B: 17   C: 19

4. *Apollo 11* took off from which space center?

   A: John F. Kennedy Space Center
   B: Lyndon B. Johnson Space Center
   C: John C. Stennis Space Center

5. What was the name of the third member of the *Apollo 11* crew, who stayed in orbit around the Moon while Neil Armstrong and Buzz Aldrin made the first crewed landing?

   A: Jim Lovell   B: Michael Collins   C: Pete Conrad

6. Many of the Moon's mountain ranges have been named after their counterparts on Earth but which one is incorrect?

   A: Montes Alpes   B: Montes Pennines
   C: Montes Pyrenaeus

7. The Moon is the largest planetary satellite in the Solar System. True or False?

8. Buzz Aldrin's mother's maiden name is Moon. True or False?

YURI GAGARIN

THE FIRST PERSON
IN SPACE

Yuri Gagarin (1934–1968) was a pilot and cosmonaut from the Soviet Union who, on 12th April 1961, became the first person to journey into outer space and the first to orbit Earth. The spacecraft, *Vostok 1*, took only 108 minutes to complete its circumnavigation of the globe. The Soviets had won round two of the Space Race, having achieved the first successful satellite launch with *Sputnik 1* in October 1957. The first American in outer space was Alan Shepard just a few weeks after Gagarin.

Gagarin was honoured around the world with awards after his safe return to Earth and became an international icon. He died aged 34 when the training jet he was flying crashed near the town of Kirzhach in western Russia. His remains were buried in the walls of the Kremlin in Moscow.

FASCINATING FACT: Unlike later Soviet space vehicles, *Vostok 1* did not have thrusters to help it slow down, so Gagarin ejected at a height of 7,000m. However, in order to qualify as a successful manned mission to space, it needed to involve a manned landing, so the Soviets concealed the truth about how Gagarin returned to Earth.

Can you name the first 20 countries, or former countries, to send people into space from the clues below?

DATE OF LAUNCH	CLUE	COUNTRY
12th April 1961	n/a	Soviet Union
5th May 1961	n/a	United States of America
2nd March 1978	Former name for the country that deposed its government during the Velvet Revolution in 1993	
27th June 1978	Central European country whose cryptologists performed a vital role in cracking the German Enigma codes during the Second World War	
26th August 1978	Former country that was formed from the Soviet Occupation Zone in the wake of the Second World War	
10th April 1979	European country bordering the Black Sea to the east and Romania to the north	
26th May 1980	The Danube runs through this country's capital, Budapest	
23rd July 1980	Southeastern country containing the Mekong Delta	

DATE OF LAUNCH	CLUE	COUNTRY
13th September 1980	The most populous country in the Caribbean	
22nd March 1981	Genghis Khan is considered this country's founding father	
14th May 1981	Contains the historical region of Transylvania	
24th June 1982	Country that famously underwent a bloody revolution from 1789 to 1799 that overthrew the monarchy	
28th November 1983	Former country who won the FIFA World Cup in 1990 while undergoing reunification	
3rd April 1984	The most populous democracy in the world	
5th October 1984	The world's second largest country by total area	
17th June 1985	Country containing both the holy cities of Mecca and Medina	
30th October 1985	Country with the largest port in Europe	
26th November 1985	Country whose flag features a coat of arms with an eagle sitting on a cactus devouring a serpent	
22nd July 1987	Arab state whose capital gets its name from a variety of cotton fabric known for its exquisite patterns	
29th August 1988	Landlocked Asian country that declared independence from Britain in 1919	

SYLVIA EARLE

QUEEN OF THE DEEP

Sylvia Earle (1935–) is an American oceanographer, diver and explorer who broke the women's world record for the deepest untethered dive in 1979, reaching 381m (1,250ft) in a specialised diving suit. Earle also tied the existing world record in 1986 for the deepest solo dive in a submarine, reaching 1,000m (3,280ft) in *Deep Rover*, a research vessel that Earle and her then-husband Graham Hawkes had designed.

In addition to leading over 50 expeditions and clocking up more than 7,000 hours underwater, Sylvia Earle is a passionate advocate for the preservation of the world's oceans. In 2009, after winning the TED prize, she founded the marine conservation organisation Mission Blue, which has set up a network of marine protected areas around the world, known as 'Hope Spots'.

On the map overleaf, can you pinpoint the positions of the
five notable low points on earth?

1. **Baku**, the lowest-lying national capital

2. **The Dead Sea**, the lowest point on land

3. **Badwater Basin, Death Valley**, the lowest point on
   land in North America

4. **Lake Assal, Djibouti**, the lowest point on land in
   Africa

5. (Really Tricky One!) **Challenger Deep**, the deepest
   point in the Earth's oceans

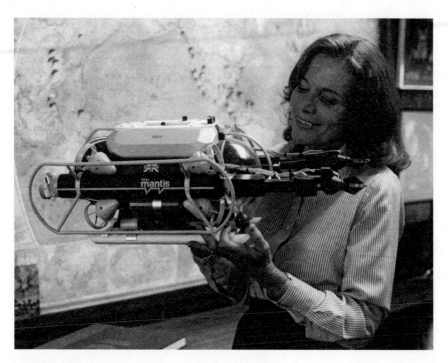

Sylvia Earle with her deep sea exploration vehicle prototype.

0   1000   2000   3000   4000   5000 miles

0   1000   2000   3000   4000   5000 km

JUNKO TABEI

MOUNTAINEERING LEGEND

Junko Tabei (1939–2016) was a Japanese mountaineer who became the first woman to reach the summit of Mount Everest. By 1992, she had climbed all of the Seven Summits – the highest mountains on each continent – and was the first woman to achieve this feat. She went on to attempt the highest mountain in every country in the world and ticked over 70 off her list. Tabei became an environmental advocate later in life working to preserve mountain environments, and she helped to build an incinerator to burn the vast amount of rubbish left by climbers on Everest.

FASCINATING FACT: In early May 1975, Tabei's expedition group camp was struck by an avalanche at 6,300m, burying the five climbers under the snow. Fortunately, everyone survived this near disaster and the sherpas were able to drag them out by their ankles. Just 11 days later, they made it to Everest's summit.

Match the mountain to the country it is situated in:

Mountains	Country
Ben Nevis	Brazil
Mount Logan	Tanzania
Mount Olympus	Indonesia
Mount Kenya	Australia
Kilimanjaro	Canada
Mount Ararat	Mexico
Elbrus	New Zealand
Aoraki (Mount Cook)	Russia
Puncak Jaya	Greece
Mount Kosciuszko	Kenya
Grossglockner	United States of America
Pico da Neblina	United Kingdom
Pico Bolívar	Austria
Denali (Mount McKinley)	Venezuela
Pico de Orizaba (Citlaltépetl)	Turkey

THE COLLECTIONS

QUIZ 3

JOHN C FRÉMONT

THE PATHFINDER

John C. Frémont (1813–1890) was a military officer and explorer, who led five expeditions to explore the American West, during which he carried out land surveys, produced maps and collected botanical and geological data. He was the first American to map the Great Salt Lake, Lake Utah and the mountains of the Sierra Nevada, where Gold Rush settlers would later extract gold worth millions of dollars. He was instrumental in the conquest of California during the Mexican-American War (1846–1848), and in 1849, he was elected as one of the first two senators from the newly formed state. Four years later, he embarked on his final expedition, successfully completing a winter passage across the mountainous west.

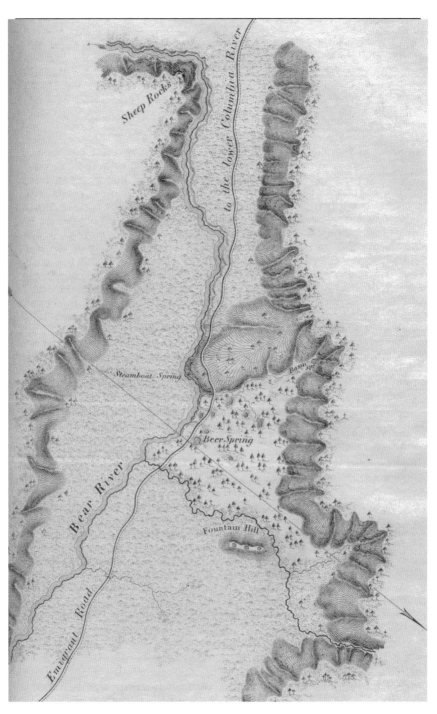

A map from 'Report of the exploring expedition to the Rocky Mountains in 1842',
by J.C. Frémont, 1845.

Which cities, all of which existed as settlements by the time of Frémont's final expedition, are being described here?

1. Founded on 29th June 1776 by Spanish colonists who named it after Saint Francis of Assisi.

2. Founded on 4th September 1781 by 44 settlers known as 'Los Pobladores' ('The townspeople'). By 1930, there were over a million inhabitants.

3. This city was the first European settlement in California, which was established on 16th July 1769. It's now home to the most-visited zoo in the USA.

4. The longest serving and highest altitude state capital, which was founded in 1610 as the capital of Nuevo Mexico.

5. A fur trading post on the northern bank of the Columbia river in the south-west corner of British Columbia, which was named after a British Royal Navy officer.

6. Founded on 27th February 1850, this city, now the state capital of California, was named by Spanish cavalry officer Gabriel Moraga after the Catholic Eucharist.

7. Originally called Bellevue, which became a suburb of a much larger city, which shares its name with one of the D-Day Landing Beaches in Normandy.

Ten features of the map below are missing. Can you add the correct label to the box provided?

Mount St Helens

Mount Hood

Great Salt Lake

San Francisco

Los Angeles

Vancouver (then called Fort Vancouver)

Omaha, Nebraska (then called Bellevue)

Kansas City (originally Westport, which was annexed by Kansas City in 1897)

Missouri River

Columbia River

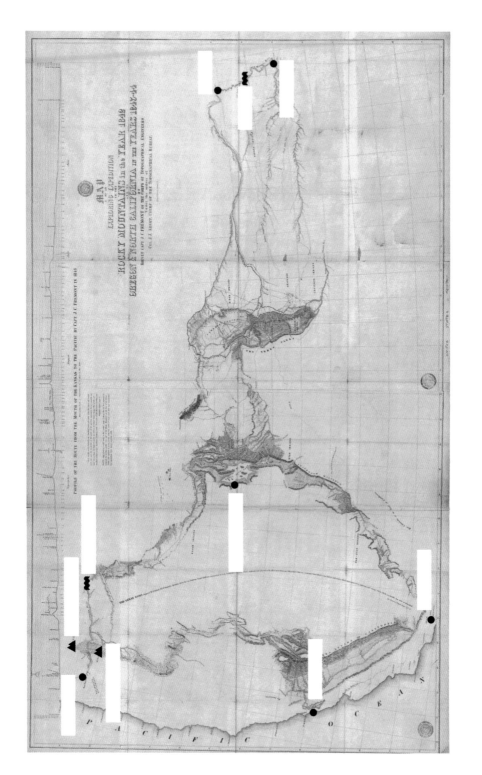

NILS ADOLF ERIK NORDENSKIÖLD

CONQUERING THE NORTHEAST PASSAGE

Nils Adolf Erik Nordenskiöld (1832–1901) was a Swedish explorer and scientist who famously completed the first navigation of the Northeast Passage. The Northeast Passage was first proposed as a trade route in the 11th century, potentially providing a quick way to travel between the Atlantic and Pacific Oceans, but it wasn't until Nordenskiöld's *Vega* expedition of 1878–1880 that the feat was finally achieved. It was also the first voyage to successfully circumnavigate Eurasia.

The scientific research from the *Vega* expedition had a pronounced effect on the understanding of climate patterns and Nordenskiöld's influential collection of maps and atlases later earned him the nickname 'the father of the history of cartography'.

Can you add the missing labels to the map for the following

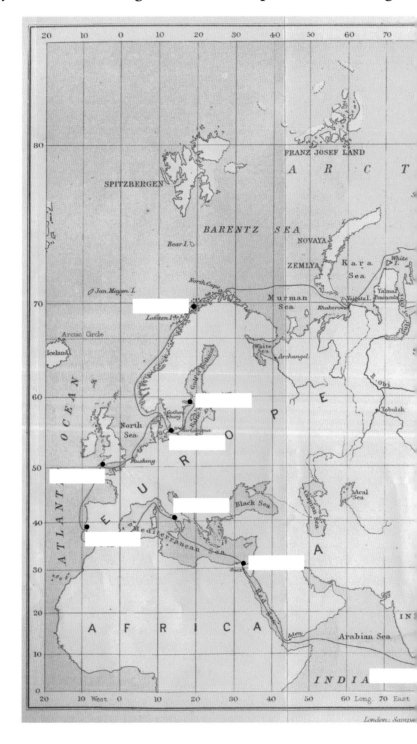

places that the *Vega* expedition stopped at along the way?

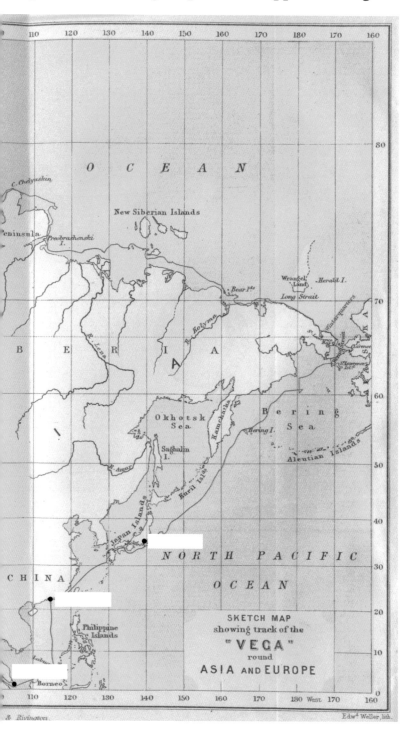

110 120 130 140 150 160 170 180 170 160

O C E A N

80

C. Chelyuskin

New Siberian Islands

eninsula   Preobrashenski
I.

Wrangel   Herald I.
Land

Bear I^te   Long Strait

70

Kolyma

B   E   R   I   A

Clarence

Okhotsk
Sea

Bering

60

Kamchatka

Bering I.   Sea

Saghalin
I.

Aleutian Islands

50

Amur

Kuril Isld

40

Japan Islands

N O R T H   P A C I F I C

CHINA

30

O C E A N

20

Philippine
Islands

SKETCH MAP
showing track of the

" V E G A "
round

ASIA AND EUROPE

10

Borneo

110 120 130 140 150 160 170 180 West 170 160   0

& Rivington.

Edwd Weller, lith.

Which Arctic creatures is Nordenskiöld describing in his book *The Voyage of the Vega around Asia and Europe?*

1. 'They not only ate up everything that was at all eatable that was left in the open air, but forced their way as well by day as by night into the houses and carried off all that they could, even such things as were of no use whatever to them, as knives, sticks, sacks, shoes and stockings . . . They nosed the noses of the sleepers to find out whether they were dead or living, and attempted to nibble at any who held their breath'

2. '. . . occurs principally on coasts and islands which are surrounded by drift-ice, often even upon ice-fields far out at sea, for his best hunting is among the ice-floes.'

3. 'In fact, the marking of this bird of prey is so similar to that of its victim that the latter can scarcely perhaps know how to take care of itself . . . It commonly sits immoveable on an open mountain slope, visible at a great distance, from the strong contrast of its white colour with the greyish-green ground. Even, in the brightest sunshine . . . it sees exceedingly well.'

4. 'During summer it betakes itself to the grassy plains in the ice-free valleys of the island, in late autumn it withdraws . . . to the sea-coast, in order to eat the seaweed that is thrown up on the beach, and in winter it goes back to the lichen-clad mountain heights in the interior of the country, where it appears to thrive exceedingly well'

5. '. . . distinguished by its long and valuable horn projecting in the longitudinal direction of the body from the upper jaw, now occurs so seldom on the coast of Novaya Zemlya that it has never been seen there by the Norwegian walrus-hunters'

6. 'A new *find* was made in 1839 . . . uncovered by a landslip on the shore of a large lake to the west of the mouth of the Yenisej, seventy versts from the Polar Sea. It was originally almost entire, so that even the trunk appears to have been preserved, to judge by the statement of the natives that a black tongue as long as a month-old reindeer calf was hanging out of the mouth'

7. What phenomenon is being described here?
'. . . at the same time cosmic and terrestrial, which on the one hand is confined within the atmosphere of our globe and stands in close connection with terrestrial magnetism, and on the other side is dependent on certain changes in the envelope of the sun, the nature of which is as yet little known, and which are indicated by the formation of spots on the sun'

FREYA STARK

PROLIFIC TRAVEL WRITER
AND PIONEERING EXPLORER
OF SOUTHERN ARABIA

Freya Stark (1893–1993) was an Anglo-Italian explorer and prolific travel writer. During the First World War, she served as a nurse in Bologna, Italy. After the war she studied Arabic at London's School of Oriental Studies. In 1927, Freya set off on her first major journey to Beirut.

By 1931, she had undertaken three treks into the wilderness of Iran, parts of which no westerner had ever traversed before. Her first travel book was published in 1932, and the following year, the Royal Geographical Society awarded her a grant to travel to Luristan and northern Persia. In 1934, she travelled to the Hadhramaut in southern Arabia to trace the ancient frankincense route, venturing farther than any westerner before her. She was trained in cartography by officials at the RGS and drew up the uncharted lands of the Lurs and made significant corrections to British Foreign Office maps.

Aged 75, Freya undertook her last expedition to Afghanistan, and continued to prepare selections of her letters well into her nineties.

Freya Stark travelled extensively across the Middle East. Can you match the modern-day state's flag with the name of the country?

Iraq	Kuwait	Turkey
Iran	Syria	Saudi Arabia
Israel	Yemen	Palestine
Lebanon	Egypt	Jordan

Junko Tabei stands against the background of the southern wall of Mount Everest with her sherpa guide Ang Tsering.

RANULPH FIENNES

'THE GREATEST LIVING EXPLORER'

'Ran' Fiennes (1944–) is a British explorer and former army officer who has made several landmark achievements in the history of exploration. After seven years of preparation, he embarked upon the Transglobe Expedition in 1979 with two former members of the Special Air Service (SAS), in an attempt to reach the South and North Poles while travelling as close to the Greenwich Meridian as possible by land and sea. In all, the journey took three years, covering approximately 52,000 miles (84,000km). His endeavours have raised millions for charity and he was named as the 'World's Greatest Living Explorer' in 1984 by the *Guinness Book of World Records*.

> **FASCINATING FACT:** In 2000, during an attempt to walk unsupported to the North Pole, he developed extreme frostbite to the fingers on his left hand and had to abandon his expedition. He was advised to postpone amputation by his surgeon to allow healthy tissue to regrow. However, suffering from constant pain that was making him 'irritable' according to his wife, Ginny, he removed the fingertips himself with a saw.

Separating fact from fiction. There are two falsehoods among the extraordinary facts below. Can you spot them?

He is the oldest Briton to reach the summit of Everest.

His first attempt to climb Everest ended in a heart attack 1,000ft from the summit.

He is the only person to cross both polar ice caps and climb the highest mountain on earth.

On his way to an event at the Royal Geographical Society in 2003, he was arrested by the Metropolitan Police for carrying an ice pick on the London Underground.

He was the youngest captain in the British Army.

Before Sir Ranulph Fiennes completed his SAS training, he was caught trying to blow up a dam 20th Century Fox had built for the film *Doctor Dolittle*.

In 2003, he ran seven marathons in seven days on seven continents.

He is scared of heights

In 1981, while trekking across Queen Elizabeth Land in Antarctica, he wrestled a young female polar bear who had entered his tent.

Fiennes's father, Lieutenant Colonel Sir Ranulph Twisleton-Wykeham-Fiennes, died four months before his son was born, after standing on a landmine while serving with the Royal Scots Greys regiment, in Italy in 1943.

In 1993, Sir Ranulph Fiennes and Dr Mike Stroud became the first people to complete an unsupported crossing of the Antartic continent on foot.

He was on the shortlist to replace George Lazenby as James Bond but was summarily rejected by producer Cubby Broccoli, who said of Fiennes, 'This one looks like a farmer. Look at his hands.'

He suffers from defective vision after his eyeball froze on a polar trek.

Fiennes in figures: Can you match the number to the fact?

3
10
13
24
65
97
94
130
156

[ ] Age when he reached the summit of Everest

[ ] The number of days it took Sir Ranulph Fiennes to walk across Antarctica

[ ] The position Sir Ranulph Fiennes appeared on the *Daily Telegraph*'s list of Top 100 Living Geniuses

[ ] The number of beats per minute his cardiac surgeon warned him not to exceed during his seven marathons in seven days challenge

[ ] The number of times doctors attempted to restart his heart after a heart attack in 2003

[ ] The number of miles he ran in the Marathon des Sables –

an annual ultra-marathon in the Sahara Desert –
in 2015

☐ The number of books Sir Ranulph Fiennes has
written

☐ The number of UK universities to present him with
an honorary doctorate or fellowship

☐ The number of attempts it took Sir Ranulph Fiennes
to scale Everest

ELLEN MACARTHUR

RECORD-BREAKING SAILOR

Dame Ellen MacArthur (1976–) is an English sailor who completed the fastest solo circumnavigation of the world in her 75ft trimaran, *B&Q*, on 7th February 2005. The previous record had been broken just nine months before Ellen's attempt by Frenchman Francis Joyon, and Ellen then beat his new record by 1 day, 8 hours, 35 minutes and 49 seconds – completing the feat in 71 days, 14 hours, 18 minutes and 33 seconds. She also finished second in the Vendée Globe solo race in 2001. Aged 24, she was the youngest person to complete the race. Shortly after completing her epic voyage, the 28-year-old Ellen was made a Dame, the youngest person in modern history to be awarded that honour.

> **FASCINATING FACT:** On Day 39 of her circumnavigation, Ellen suffered a severe burn to her arm on the exhaust of a generator. She continued on and three days later she completed her fastest 24-hour run, covering 501.6 miles (807.2km) before rounding Cape Horn.

Can you fill in the missing words from Ellen's diaries during her 2001 Vendée Globe race and her 2005 circumnavigation?

1. **(Day 25, 2005 circumnavigation)**: 'I've got a real problem. I've gone off _____ and, unfortunately, I based my diet on eating a lot of them. Worse than that, I've gone off _____ as well.'

   A: Muesli bars/porridge   B: Sardines/canned tuna
   C: Baked beans/bananas

2. **(Day 40, 2005 circumnavigation)**: 'My body has been pushed beyond its limits, and once again I found myself screaming at the heavens . . . I apologise to the _____ that came closer in wonder at what my cries were all about.'

   A: Seagull   B: Albatross   C: Pigeon

3. **(Day 55, 2005 circumnavigation)**: 'I feel like I've been beaten up, stiff as hell and moving around with the speed and elegance of _____'

   A: A rusty oil tanker   B: An arthritic robot
   C: An old tortoise

4. **(Day 16, 2005 circumnavigation)**: 'I crossed the equator at 01:25 GMT – celebrated with a bottle of _____, most of it went on the boat not me – on purpose. I thanked _____ for letting us pass…'

A: Rum/God   B: Wine/the heavens
C: Champagne/Neptune

5. **(Day 3, 2001 Vendée Globe race)**: 'Spoke to my
   uncle [a GP] today, to ask him if I should stick a
   _____ through my fingernail to release a
   bit of pressure as it was black after I trapped it while
   trying to open a ballast valve last night. The answer
   was _____.'

   A: Burning hot wire/Yes   B: Toothpick/No
   C: Needle/Yes

6. **(Day 56, 2001 Vendée Globe race)**: 'We made
   it and I was then faced with the most beautiful
   iceberg I could imagine. Wide, blue, high-arched
   caves, and a height that must have been similar to
   _____.'

   A: Nelson's Column   B: The White Cliffs of Dover
   C: Big Ben

7. **(Day 72, 2001 Vendée Globe race)**: 'Yesterday I
   dreamt _____ was on board, but I've no idea
   why. If someone could find out whether he likes milk
   in his coffee, and how much, that would be great – I'd
   love to know if my dream was factually correct or not!'

   A: Richard Branson   B: Ranulph Fiennes
   C: David Attenborough

FELICITY ASTON

GROUNDBREAKING
POLAR EXPLORER

Felicity Aston (1977–) is an English explorer and former meteorologist for the British Antarctic Survey. In November 2011–January 2012, she became the first person to travel across Antarctica using muscle power alone – a journey of 1,744km (1,084 miles) that took her 59 days on skis. She pulled two sleds that weighed a combined 190lbs (86kg).

Felicity also led the first British women's crossing of Greenland and the largest international women's team to ski to the South Pole.

FASCINATING FACT: In 2015, 37-year-old Felicity was awarded the Polar Medal – becoming the youngest female recipient – and received an MBE from Her Majesty the Queen for her services to polar exploration.

Gifted by the Sovereign of the United Kingdom, the Polar Medal was first awarded in 1904. It was originally known as the Arctic Medal and honours 'extreme human endeavour against the appalling weather and conditions that exist in the Arctic and Antarctic'.

Can you work out the other recipients of the Polar Medal from the clues below?

1. Leader of the ill-fated *Terra Nova* expedition of 1910–1913.

2. English explorer who led the Commonwealth Trans-Antarctic Expedition, which completed the first overland crossing of Antarctica in 1958.

3. A distant relative of the Queen and the first man to complete the first unsupported crossing of the Antarctic continent (along with Mike Stroud).

4. New Zealander who achieved his most epic feat on 29th May 1953.

5. Explorer who sailed the *James Caird* approximately 800 miles to save the lives of the stranded members of his Imperial Trans-Antarctic Expedition of 1914–1917.

6. The mastermind behind her husband's polar treks and a pioneering researcher for the British Antarctic Survey, she was the first woman to be awarded the medal and the first woman to be invited to join the Antarctic Club.

7. Pioneering climate scientist, current director of the British Antarctic Survey, and the Chancellor of the University of Leeds.

8. A fictional recipient of the medal noted for his 'We're doomed' catchphrase while serving in the Walmington-on-Sea Home Guard.

LEVISON WOOD

WALKING THE WORLD

Levison Wood (1982–) is an English ex-paratrooper and explorer renowned for his long walking expeditions. From 2013–2014, he set out to walk the length of the River Nile – a distance of 4,250 miles. In 2015, he travelled the length of the Himalayas – a journey of over 1,700 miles. In 2017, he walked along the length of Central America, venturing across eight countries and traversing the legendary Darién Gap – an area of almost impenetrable jungle. Later that year, he undertook a full circumnavigation of the Arabian Peninsula, covering a distance of 5,000 miles.

Walking the Nile: Can you fill in the name of the six countries Levison travelled to during his journey?

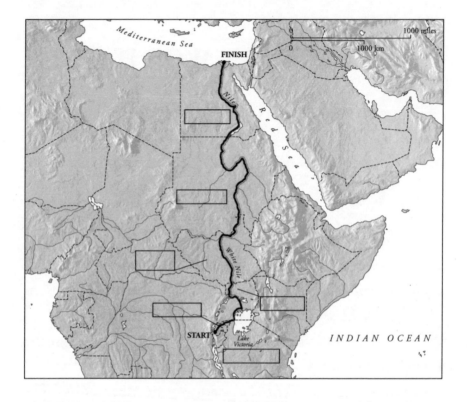

FASCINATING FACT: Levison Wood is known for politely accepting offers to feast in regional delicacies. During his travels, he's eaten goat's eye "alright actually – a bit like jelly" and brain "horrible like a pâte or something" in Afghanistan. In Uganda, he wolfed down a bowl of what seemed like beans and rice before finding out from his guide that the grains of 'rice' were actually maggots.

Walking the Americas: Can you fill in the name of the eight countries Levison travelled to during his journey?

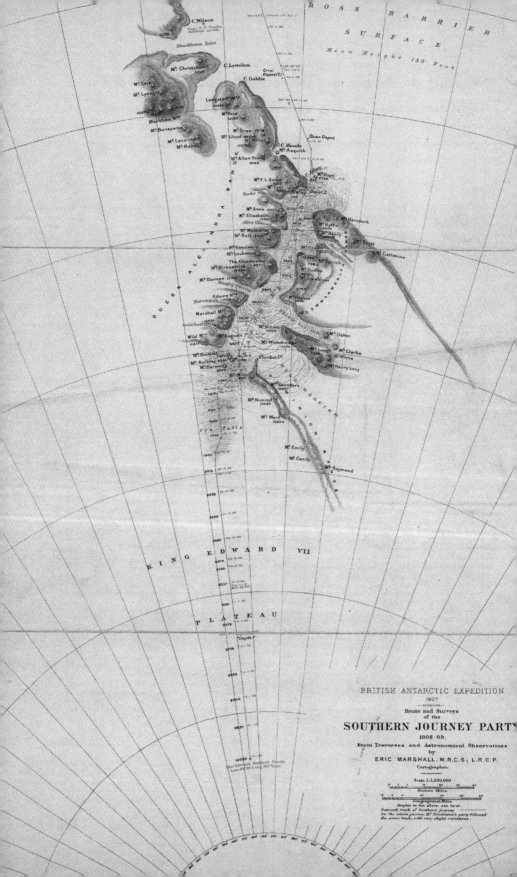

ROSS BARRIER SURFACE

Mean Height 150 Feet

C. Wilson

Shackleton Inlet

Mt Christchurch
C. Lyttelton
C. Goldie
Crisi Depot (C.)

Mt Carr
Mt Lysaght
Longstaff Mts
Mt Reid

Markham Mts
Mt Bonaparte
Mt Tripp
Quan Depot

Mt Leeatner
Mt Rabot
Mt Lloyd
Mt Miller
C. Maude
Mt Asquith

Mt Allen Young
C. Allen

Mt Hope
C. Alice

Mt F. L. Smith
Depot D
Mt Fox
Socks Glr.

Mt Anne
Mt Harcourt
Mt Elizabeth
Mt Kyffin
Mt Henry
Alice Glacier
Mt Mackellar
Mt Bell
Mt Scott
Mt Catherine

Mt Stanley
Mt Lockwood
Mt Patrick
The Cloudmaker
Mt Kirkpatrick
Mt Dudley
Mt Dorman
Bingley
Mt Donaldson

Adams Mts
Barwick Gl.
Mt Deakin

Marshall Mts
Swinford Gl.
Mt Kinsey
Mt Usher

Wild Mts
Mt Augusta
Mt Westminster
Mt Clarke
Mt Buckley
Mt Iveagh
Mt Darwin
Mt White
Plunket Pt.
Mt Henry Lucy

Mt Mill
Mt Saunders

Mt Nimrod

Ice Falls
Mt Ward

Mt Emily
Mt Cecily
Mt Raymond

KING EDWARD VII

PLATEAU

Depot F

Shackleton's furthest South
Lat. 88° 23 Long. 162° East

BRITISH ANTARCTIC EXPEDITION
1907

Route and Surveys
of the

SOUTHERN JOURNEY PARTY
1908-09.

From Traverses and Astronomical Observations
by

ERIC MARSHALL, M.R.C.S., L.R.C.P.
Cartographer.

Scale 1:1,500,000

Statute Miles

Geographical Miles

Heights in feet above sea-level.
Outward track of Southern journey
On the return journey Mr Shackleton's party followed
the same track, with very slight variations.

THE ROYAL
GEOGRAPHICAL SOCIETY
FAMILY QUIZ

1. Match the description of a Christmas meal in the Antarctic to the explorer

(i) 'We had four courses. The first, pemmican, full whack, with slices of horse meat flavoured with onion and curry powder and thickened with biscuit; then an arrowroot, cocoa and biscuit hoosh sweetened; then a plum-pudding; then cocoa with raisins, and finally a dessert of caramels and ginger. After the feast it was difficult to move. Wilson and I couldn't finish our share of plum-pudding.'

(ii) 'We could not carry it all with us, so for the last time for eight months we had a really good meal – as much as we could eat. Anchovies in oil, baked beans, and jugged hare made a glorious mixture such as we have not dreamed of since our school-days.'

(iii) 'The tent was raised at 9.30am. after a run of eleven miles one hundred and seventy-six yards. An ounce each of butter was served out from our small stock to give a festive touch to the dog-stew.'

(iv) 'All crumbs of biscuit were carefully collected by Wisting, the cook for the day, and put into a bag. This was taken into the tent and vigorously beaten and kneaded; the result was pulverized biscuit. With this product and a sausage of dried milk, Wisting succeeded in making a capital dish of Christmas porridge.'

A: Douglas Mawson, 1912
B: Ernest Shackleton, 1915
C: Roald Amundsen, 1912
D: Robert Falcon Scott, 1911

2. Christmas Island is an external territory in the Indian Ocean administered by which country?

A: India   B: New Zealand   C: Australia

3. There are over a dozen little towns of Bethlehem in the USA. Can you name the states they are situated in from the clues?

A: This state shares part of its name with a famous New York railway station
B: The state that plays host to the US Masters golf tournament

C: New England state with the motto 'Live Free or Die'
D: State named in honour of King Charles I of England
and site of the first successful heavier-than-air flight
by the Wright Brothers

**4. Charles Dickens's *A Christmas Carol* is set in
which city?**

A: London, England   B: Dublin, Ireland
C: Edinburgh, Scotland

**5. Who was the first European to reach India by sea, a feat
achieved on his voyage of 1497–1499?**

A: Christopher Columbus   B: Vasco da Gama
C: Marco Polo

**6. Which French naval officer, explorer and conservationist
co-invented the 'Aqua-Lung'?**

7. What is 'Buzz' Aldrin's first name?

A: Edward   B: Eddard   C: Edwin

8. How many countries in the world begin with 'Saint'?

**9. There are numerous replicas of the Statue of Liberty on
display around the world. Can you work out the
location from the clues?**

A: The city where the original statue was constructed

B: Sixth-largest French city, located in the Nouvelle-Aquitaine region

C: USA city with a Spanish name that translates as 'The Meadows'

D: City watched over by Christ the Redeemer

10. Which famous church began construction in 1882 and is not due to be completed until at least 2030?

11. In which city can you find a bronze statue of The Little Mermaid, the character created in a fairytale by Hans Christian Andersen?

12. American-Chinese architect I. M. Pei famously designed the entrance to which museum in the 1980s, triggering many years of debate?

A: The Hermitage, St Petersburg   B: National Museum of Natural History, Washington D.C.

C: The Louvre, Paris

13. Victor Lustig was a legendary scam artist, who managed to 'sell' which monument in the 1920s?

A: The Eiffel Tower, Paris   B: The Colosseum, Rome

C: Big Ben, London

14. What is the common name for the tectonic boundary between the Pacific plate and the North American plate?

15. What are the names of the four main islands of Japan?

16. Name all the countries in the world that begin with the letter 'R' (there are three).

17. Easter Island is a 'special territory' administered by the government of which country?

    A: Argentina   B: Ecuador   C: Chile

18. In 1994, the American Society of Civil Engineers made a list of Seven Engineering Wonders of the Modern World. Can you work out four of them from the clues?

    A: The tunnel with the longest undersea section in the world

    B: The tallest structure in the world from 1931 to 1954

    C: The largest hydroelectric facility at the time, but beaten into second place by the Three Gorges Dam in China in 2012

    D: Waterway connecting the two largest oceans in the world

19. On the Beaufort Scale, a 'hurricane' is deemed to have a wind strength of at least which speed?

    A: 73mph   B: 83mph   C: 93mph

20. The World Heritage Site stretching from Exmouth, East Devon to Studland Bay in Dorset, UK is known by which name?

> A: Cretaceous Coast   B: Jurassic Coast
> C: Triassic Coast

21. Match the city's nickname with the city

> (i) The Eternal City   A: Dubrovnik
> (ii) The Fair City   B: New Orleans
> (iii) The Lion City   C: Rome
> (iv) The Forbidden City   D: Dublin
> (v) The Pearl of the Adriatic   E: Singapore
> (vi) The Big Easy   F: Beijing

22. Which countries share the longest land border in the world?

> A: Canada and the USA   B: Kazakhstan and Russia
> C: Chile and Argentina

23. The Volga river empties into which body of water?

> A: The Aral Sea   B: The Black Sea
> C: The Caspian Sea

24. Name the 10 countries the Danube river flows through or borders:

A _ _ _ _ _ _
B _ _ _ _ _ _ _
C _ _ _ _ _ _
G _ _ _ _ _ _
H _ _ _ _ _ _
M _ _ _ _ _ _
R _ _ _ _ _ _
S _ _ _ _ _
S _ _ _ _ _ _ _
U _ _ _ _ _ _

25. Name the 10 states that the Mississippi river flows through or borders:

A _ _ _ _ _ _ _
I _ _ _ _ _ _ _
I _ _ _
K _ _ _ _ _ _ _
L _ _ _ _ _ _ _ _
M _ _ _ _ _ _ _ _ _ _
M _ _ _ _ _ _ _ _
M _ _ _ _ _ _ _
T _ _ _ _ _ _ _ _
W _ _ _ _ _ _ _ _

26. In terms of elevation, what is the highest capital city in the world?

A: Kathmandu, Nepal   B: Thimphu, Bhutan
C: La Paz, Bolivia

27. After Baku, Azerbaijan, which is the second lowest-lying national capital?

A: Amsterdam, Netherlands
B: Bandar Seri Begawan, Brunei
C: Washington DC, USA

28. Old Faithful is a famous geyser located in which national park?

A: Yosemite   B: Yellowstone   C: Grand Canyon

29. After the flag of the United States of America, which country features the most stars on it?

A: Uzbekistan   B: Brazil   C: Honduras

30. Which two countries have almost identical flags, with a red horizontal stripe sitting over a white horizontal stripe?

A: Poland and Monaco   B: Poland and Indonesia
C: Monaco and Indonesia

31. Which conquistador led the Spanish conquest of the Inca Empire?

A: Hernán Cortes   B: Francisco Pizarro
C: Francisco de Orellana

32. What unites the cities of Brasilia, Abuja, Canberra, Islamabad and Naypyidaw?

33. Which desert, believed to be the oldest on earth, is situated between the Andes mountains and the Cordillera de la Costa mountain range?

A: Mojave Desert   B: Black Rock Desert
C: Atacama Desert

34. Victoria Falls is a waterfall in southern Africa situated on which river?

A: The Zambezi   B: The Nile   C: The Congo

35. In which state would you find Denali, also known as Mount McKinley?

A: Alaska   B: Montana   B: Washington

36. The four Tennis Grand Slam tournaments are held in the cities of London, England; Paris, France; New York, USA and which other city/country?

37. Which is the only city that has held three Summer Olympic games?

38. Only five capitals begin with the letter B and contain eight letters. Name those capitals!

B _ _ _ _ _ _ _

B _ _ _ _ _ _ _

B _ _ _ _ _ _ _

B _ _ _ _ _ _ _

B _ _ _ _ _ _ _

39. Only one capital city starts with the letter E, I, Q, U or Z. Name those capitals!

I _ _ _ _ _ _ _ _

Q _ _ _ _

U _ _ _ _ _ _ _ _ _ _

Z _ _ _ _ _

40.–50. Can you colour in the following countries on the blank map of the world over the page?

(i) Finland

(ii) Mongolia

(iii) Poland

(iv) Bolivia

(v) Afghanistan

(vi) Botswana

(vii) Chad

(viii) Vietnam

(ix) Oman

(x) Papua New Guinea

(xi) Suriname

0 1000 2000 3000 4000 5000 miles
0 1000 2000 3000 4000 5000 km

ANSWERS

FOREWORD PUZZLE

SatyR

LatakiA   (tobacco and port)

EveresT

D------I   (as in Di for the goddess Diana)

GrottO

EveN

MARCO POLO – FOLLOWING THE SILK ROAD TO XANADU (Page 3)

1. *Citizen Kane*
2. The Golden Raspberries or Razzies
3. DC Comics
4. Saturn
5. Bill Gates

BRAINTEASER: Samuel Taylor Coleridge

'I have only told you half of what I saw'
  1. Elephant
  2. Crocodile
  3. Rhinoceros
  4. Salt
  5. Japan

ZHENG HE – INTREPID MING DYNASTY EXPLORER (p.9)

1. Jeddah ('Jed' – da)
2. Mombasa (Mom – basa)
3. Mogadishu (Mog–add–ischoo)
4. Aden (Aid – den)
5. Maldives (Mal – dives)
6. Bangkok (Bang – cock)
7. Beijing (Bay – jing)
8. Macau (Mac – cow)
9. Nanking (Nan – king)

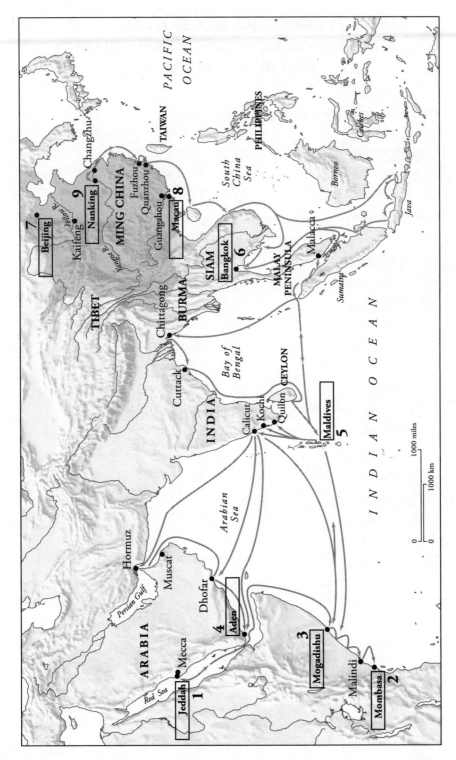

FERDINAND MAGELLAN –
THE FIRST CIRCUMNAVIGATION (NEARLY)
OF THE WORLD (p.13)

Correct order of missing words:

1. Spice Islands
2. Gulf of Cadiz
3. Canary Islands
4. Equator
5. Brazil
6. mutinied
7. anchor line
8. marooned
9. executed
10. Cape Horn
11. Tierra del Fuego
12. 38
13. Strait of Magellan
14. Sea of the South
15. scurvy
16. ox hides
17. masts
18. deserted
19. 99
20. Philippines
21. baptised
22. 50
23. 1,500
24. mirror
25. banquet
26. set alight
27. seven
28. spectacles
29. quicksilver
30. pearls
31. cinnamon
32. gold
33. Cape of Good Hope
34. starvation
35. Cape Verde
36. 18

HERNÁN CORTÉS – RUTHLESS CONQUEROR OF THE AZTEC EMPIRE (p.21)

1. B. Second cousin once removed
2. A. Lawyer
3. C. 200,000 and 300,000
4. A. Scuttled his ships
5. C. Hearts
6. B. Smallpox
7. A. Gold
8. B. Cocoa
9. C. Burning his feet
10. A. Mexico City

The Road to Tenochtitlán

1. ZEMPOALA
2. VILLA RICA DE LA VERA CRUZ
3. ZEMPOALA
4. XALAPA
5. IXHUACAN
6. IXTACAMAXTITLAN
7. TLAXCALA
8. CHOLULA
9. AMECAMECA
10. MIXQUIC
11. IZTAPALAPA
12. TENOCHTITLAN

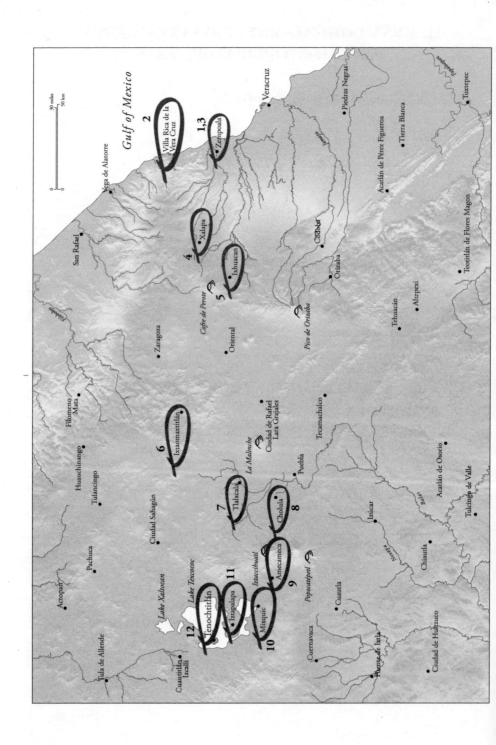

ESTEVANICO – THE TRAVELS OF AN EXTRAORDINARY SLAVE (p.29)

Answers (General Knowledge Trivia)

1. Arizona
2. Texas
3. Mississippi
4. Alabama
5. Florida
6. Louisiana
7. New Mexico (Roswell)

Answers (Music Trivia)

1. Arizona (From 1972's 'Take It Easy' by the Eagles)

2. Texas (From 1987's 'All My Ex's Live in Texas' by George Strait)

3. Mississippi (the lyrics come from 2006's 'Dani California' by the Red Hot Chili Peppers)

4. Birmingham, **Alabama** (the lyrics come from 1973's 'Sweet Home Alabama' by Lynyrd Skynyrd)

5. Miami, **Florida** (the lyrics are from Will Smith's 1997 hit 'Miami')

6. New Orleans, the most populous city in **Louisiana** (from 1964's 'House of the Rising Sun' by the Animals)

7. Albuquerque, the most populous city in **New Mexico** (from 1988's 'The King of Rock 'n' Roll' by Prefab Sprout)

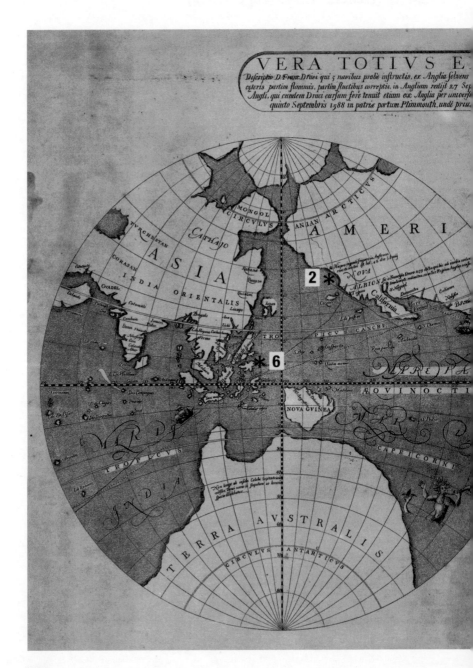

Award of Arms

(ENGLISH)

WITH DIVINE HELP

THUS GREAT THINGS FROM SMALL THINGS

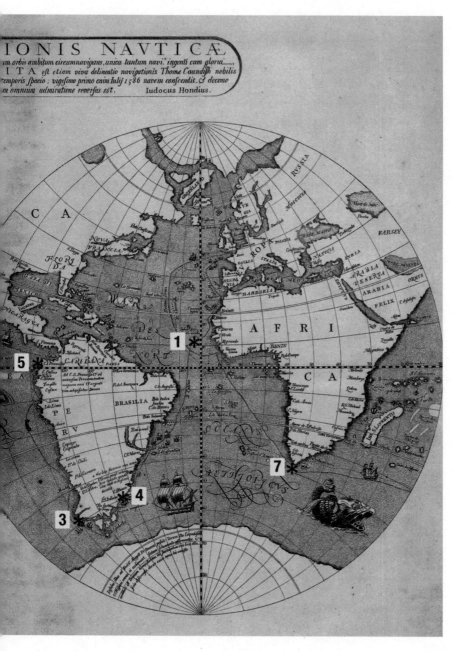

ABEL TASMAN – SEEKING THE GREAT SOUTH LAND (p.39)

1. B. Staten
2. A. Maori
3. C. Murderers' Bay
4. A. Christmas Day 1642
5. A. Fiji
6. B. Circumnavigating Australia
7. B. Old nails
8. A. Plant the Dutch flag

ABEL TASMAN – SOME MEN ARE ISLANDS

1. **Bermuda**, named after Spanish sea captain Juan de Bermúdez in 1505

2. **Cook Islands**, named in honour of English naval officer and explorer Captain James Cook (1728–1779)

3. **Lanzarote**, named after Genoese navigator Lanzerotto Malocello in the early 14th century

4. **Pitcairn Island**, named for British Royal Navy midshipman Robert Pitcairn, who spotted the island in 1767

5. **Tristan da Cunha**, named after Portuguese navigator Tristão da Cunha (*c.*1460–1540)

6. **Baffin Island**, named after English explorer William Baffin (*c.*1584–1622)

7. **Dirk Hartog Island**, named for Dirk Hartog (1580–1621) who discovered it in 1616

8. **Marshall Islands**, named after British explorer John Marshall, who visited in 1788

RENÉ-ROBERT CAVELIER SIEUR DE LA SALLE – CLAIMING 'LA LOUISIANE' FOR FRANCE (p.45)

1. Missouri
2. Mississippi
3. Colorado
4. Rio Grande
5. St Lawrence

WILLIAM DAMPIER – 'A MAN OF EXQUISITE MIND' (p.49)

1. Canary Islands
2. Cape Verde
3. Salvador
4. Cape of Good Hope
5. Timor
6. New Guinea
7. Jakarta (formerly Batavia)
8. St Helena
9. Ascension Island

BRAINTEASER: Barbecue

Dampier mentions a 'borbecu' in *A New Voyage Round the World* to refer to frames of sticks raised roughly 3ft from the ground to help prevent against snakebite. These wooden frameworks were also used to grill meat and fish.

Dampier and the Dictionary

1. Avocado
2. Lychee
3. Chopsticks
4. Cashew

BRAINTEASER: *Gulliver's Travels* **by Jonathan Swift**

William Dampier's Third Circumnavigation 1708–1711
1. 33
2. 38
3. 29
4. 78
5. 50
6. 28

(Selkirk's message reveals his coordinates as: 33° 38' 29" S 78° 50' 28" W)

BRAINTEASER: Robinson Crusoe

Daniel Defoe's character Robinson Crusoe was partly inspired by Selkirk's experience. After complaining about the seaworthiness of the ship *Cinque Ports*, captained by Thomas Stradling, Selkirk was marooned on Más a Tierra with a musket, a hatchet, a knife, a cooking pot and a Bible. He survived for four years and four months in surprisingly good health and was made second mate of the *Duke*, the ship that rescued him. Selkirk's concerns about *Cinque Ports* came to pass, as it foundered off the coast of Colombia, and the surviving crew were imprisoned.

JAMES COOK – THE MAN WHO SAILED 'AS FAR AS I THINK IT POSSIBLE FOR MAN TO GO' (p.55)

1. Kangaroo
2. Walrus
3. Penguin
4. Sting ray
5. Easter Island statues
6. Tonga
7. A drug that prevents scurvy
8. Botany Bay

12th Greatest Briton

1. Sir Winston Churchill
2. Isambard Kingdom Brunel
3. Diana, Princess of Wales
4. Charles Darwin
5. William Shakespeare
6. Sir Isaac Newton
7. Elizabeth I
8. John Lennon
9. Horatio Nelson
10. Oliver Cromwell
11. Sir Ernest Shackleton

CARSTEN NIEBUHR – A CONSCIENTIOUS EXPLORER (p.61)

A, W	Copenhagen
B	Marseille
C, T	Constantinople
D	Alexandria
E	Cairo
F	Suez
G	Jeddah
H	Mocha
I	Sana'a
J	Bombay
K	Muscat
L	Shiraz
M	Basra
N	Baghdad
O	Mosul

P, S	Aleppo
Q	Cyprus
R	Jerusalem
U	Bucharest
V	Warsaw

LA PÉROUSE –THE LOST EXPLORER
OF THE PACIFIC (p.65)

1. Taiwan
2. Hawaiian Islands
3. Tonga
4. Tahiti
5. Samoa
6. Vanuatu
7. Manitoba

ALEXANDER VON HUMBOLDT –
'THE GREATEST SCIENTIFIC TRAVELLER
WHO EVER LIVED' (p.69)

1. Alexander von Humboldt was the first person to describe
the phenomenon and cause of human-induced climate change
in 1800.

3. Alexander von Humboldt invented the term 'isotherms' to
describe the connections between different geographical points
around the world experiencing the same temperature.

4. Alexander Von Humbolt invented the term 'magnetic storms'
to refer to disturbances in Earth's magnetic field.

6. In April 1827, Alexander von Humboldt spent 40 minutes at the bottom of the River Thames in the diving bell used by the British engineer Isambard Kingdom Brunel during the construction of the Thames Tunnel.

A Pioneering Voyage

1. Jaguar
2. Toucan
3. Capybara
4. Indigo
5. Passion flower

An Enlightened Friendship

1. Illinois
2. South Dakota
3. Nebraska
4. Iowa
5. Tennessee
6. Kansas
7. Minnesota
8. Arizona
9. California
10. Nevada

MERIWETHER LEWIS AND WILLIAM CLARK – HEROES OF THE AMERICAN WEST (p.77)

Modern-day States

1. Illinois (Ill-i-noise)
2. Missouri (Miss-sour-i)
3. Kansas (Kan-SAS)
4. Iowa (Io-WA)

5. Nebraska (Né-bra-scar)
6. South Dakota (South Da-quota)
7. North Dakota
8. Montana (Mont-tanner)
9. Idaho (Id-a hoe)
10. Oregon (Ore-gone)
11. Washington (Washing-ton)

Guess the Animal

1. B. Grizzly Bear
2. C. American Badger
3. A. Prairie Dog
4. A. Wolverine
5. B. American White Pelican
6. C. Mountain Lion (Cougar)

IDA PFEIFFER – A WOMAN'S JOURNEY AROUND THE WORLD (p.83)

Man-Made Wonders

1. The Pantheon
2. The Great Sphinx of Giza
3. Pompeii
4. The Acropolis
5. The Taj Mahal
6. St Peter's Basilica
7. The Hanging Gardens of Babylon

Natural Wonders

1. Mount Etna
2. The Dead Sea
3. Mount Vesuvius
4. River Ganges
5. River Danube
6. River Nile
7. Mount Ararat

JAMES CLARK ROSS – POLAR PIONEER (p.91)

Coordinates

The coordinates are: **70°05'N, 96°46'W**

1. **70** (USA: 50, Europe: 12, Australia: 6, Ghana: 1, Vietnam: 1)

2. **5** (Nigeria: 3, Poland: 2)

3. **96** (**8** states begin with 'N': Nebraska, Nevada, New Hampshire, New Jersey, New Mexico, New York, North Carolina, North Dakota; there are **12** sovereign states in South America: Argentina, Bolivia, Brazil, Chile, Colombia, Ecuador, Guyana, Paraguay, Peru, Suriname, Uruguay, Venezuela)

4. **46** (**10** Canadian provinces: Alberta, British Columbia, Manitoba, New Brunswick, Newfoundland & Labrador, Nova Scotia, Ontario, Prince Edward Island, Quebec, Saskatchewan; multiplied by **4** African countries beginning with 'B': Benin, Botswana, Burkina Faso, Burundi; plus **5** countries bordering Switzerland: Austria, France, Germany, Italy, Liechtenstein; plus **1** country that features a gun: the flag of Mozambique features an AK-47)

The Arctic Exploration

1. *Twenty Thousand Leagues Under the Sea*
2. *Heart of Darkness*
3. Michael Palin
4. Charles Dickens
5. Mark Twain
6. Mars
7. Mount Sidley

DAVID LIVINGSTONE – MAN ON A MISSION (p.97)

TIMELINE SEQUENCE: 6, 2, 5, 8, 1, 7, 4, 3

Hall of Heroes

1. Robert the Bruce (1274–1329), formidable warrior and king of Scots

2. Robert 'Rabbie' Burns (1759–1796), the Scottish national poet

3. Adam Smith (1723–1790), economist

4. Sir Walter Scott (1771–1832), celebrated author who wrote the *Waverley* series of novels

5. James Watt (1736–1819), instrument maker and inventor who transformed steam engine efficiency

6. Thomas Carlyle (1795–1881), philosopher and social commentator

ISABELLA BIRD – PIONEERING ADVENTURER (p.103)

1. *Among the Tibetans*
2. *Unbeaten Tracks in Japan*

3. *A Lady's Life in the Rocky Mountains*
4. *The Hawaiian Archipelago*
5. *The Englishwoman in America*
6. *Journeys in Persia and Kurdistan*
7. *The Golden Chersonese and the Way Thither*
8. *Notes on Old Edinburgh*

Across:
6. Rattan
7. Singapore
8. Shintoism
10. Aloha
11. Desperado
12. Mauna Loa

Down:
1. Caravan
2. Durian
3. Mikado
4. Dervish
5. Chrysanthemum
9. Tahoe

FRIDTJOF NANSEN – FARTHEST NORTH (p.109)

DATE	EXPLORER(S)	LATITUDE	LONGITUDE
1596	William Barents	79°	49'
1707	Cornelius Giles	81°	n/a
1806	William Scoresby Sr.	81°	30'
1827	Sir William Edward Parry	82°	45'
1875	Sir Albert Hastings Markham	83°	20'
1882	Adolphus Greely	83°	24'
1895	Fridtjof Nansen	86°	14'

WILLIAM BARENTS

Latitude: HTTP code for 'Not Found' **(404) divided by** the number of lions at the base of Nelson's Column in Trafalgar Square **(4) minus** the number of plagues of Egypt in the Bible **(10) minus** the number of jurors in a criminal trial **(12)** = 79

Longitude: The number of pounds in a stone **(14) multiplied by** the number of consecutive strikes in tenpin bowling known as a 'turkey' **(3) plus** the number of hills in ancient Rome **(7)** = **49**

CORNELIS GILES

Latitude: The number of circles of hell in Dante's *Inferno* **(9) multiplied by** the number of swans a-swimming in the 'Twelve Days of Christmas' **(7) plus** the number of holes on a golf course **(18)** = **81**

WILLIAM SCORESBY SR.

Latitude: The number of stars in the EU flag **(12) multiplied by** the smallest positive integer that is neither a prime nor a square number **(6) plus** the number of Nazgûl in *The Lord of the Rings* **(9)** = **81** **Longitude:** The sum of the first three prime numbers **(10) plus** the number of numbers on a dartboard **(20)** = **30**

SIR WILLIAM EDWARD PARRY

Latitude: The address number on Pennsylvania Avenue of the White House **(1600) divided by** the number of pawns in a chess set **(16) minus** the number of yards away from the goal the edge of the penalty area is situated in soccer **(18)** = **82**

Longitude: The answer to the 'ultimate question of life, the universe and everything' according to Douglas Adams **(42) plus** the number of points awarded for a penalty in rugby union **(3)** = **45**

SIR ALBERT HASTINGS MARKHAM

Latitude: The number of miles in a marathon to the nearest whole number **(26) multiplied by** the number of Noble Truths in Buddhism **(4) minus** the minimum legal age to purchase alcohol in the USA **(21)** = **83**

Longitude: The number of lines in a sonnet **(14) plus** the number of legs insects have **(6)** = **20**

ADOLPHUS GREELY

Latitude: A platinum wedding anniversary in years **(70) plus** the number of the 'Death' card in a Tarot deck **(13)** = **83**

Longitude: The number of syllables in a traditional haiku **(17) plus** the number of books in the *Harry Potter* series **(7)** = **24**

FRIDTJOF NANSEN

Latitude: The number of the Apollo mission that first landed on the Moon **(11) multiplied by** the number of canine teeth in an adult human **(4) plus** the 'number' of Bill Clinton's presidency in the sequence of US presidents **(42)** = **86**

Longitude: The number of carats representing 100% pure gold **(24) minus** the number a boxing referee counts to in order to declare a winner by knockout **(10)** = **14**

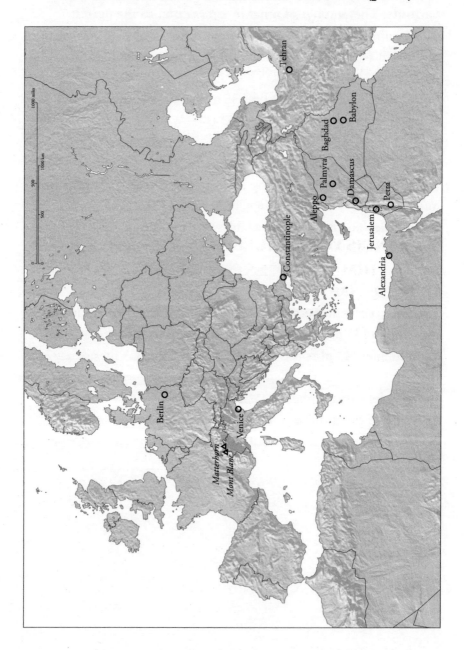

MARY KINGSLEY – A TRULY INDEPENDENT WOMAN (p.115)

1. B. shooting things with a gun
2. A. an earthen water cooler
3. C. drowning
4. A. dying
5. B. a good thick skirt
6. C. had tea
7. A. an instant hot bath

FRANCIS YOUNGHUSBAND – THE FATHER OF HIMALAYAN EXPLORATION (p.131)

HEIGHT	FIRST CONFIRMED ASCENT	CLIMBERS	MOUNTAIN?
4,884m	February 1962	Heinrich Harrer; Russell Kippax, Albert Huizenga and Phillip Temple	Puncak Jaya [Carstensz Pyramid]
4,892m	December 1966	Barry Corbet, John Evans, William Long, Peter Schoening	Vinson
5,642m	Summer 1874	Florence Crauford Grove, Frederick Gardner, Horace Walker, Peter Knubel	Elbrus [West Summit]
5,895m	October 1889	Hans Meyer and Ludwig Purtscheller	Kilimanjaro
6,194m	June 1913	Walter Harper, Harry Karstens, Hudson Stuck and Robert Tatum	Denali [Mount McKinley]
6,962m	January 1897	Matthias Zurbriggen	Aconcagua
8,848m	May 1953	Edmund Hillary and Tenzing Norgay	Everest

NELLIE BLY – AROUND THE WORLD IN (LESS THAN) 80 DAYS (p.135)

1. A. Nellie Bly went out of her way to meet Jules Verne in France during her journey and the author wished her good luck.

2. B. Nellie Bly invented and secured a patent for both a new type of milk can and a stacking garbage can.

3. C. While in Singapore, Nellie bought a monkey called McGinty, who accompanied her for the remainder of the journey.

4. A. Bly's journalistic career began with a furious response to an editorial entitled 'What Girls are Good For' in the *Pittsburgh Dispatch* in 1888 which impressed the editor so much he gave her a job.

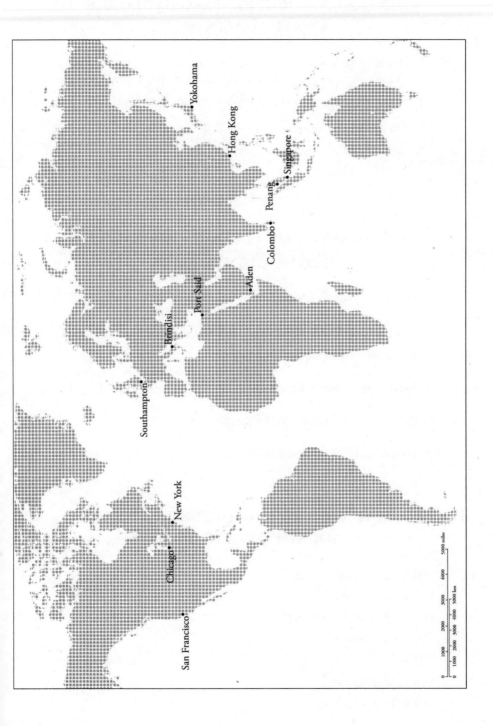

SVEN HEDIN – TRAILBLAZING EXPLORER OF CENTRAL ASIA (p.141)

1. C. Baghdad
2. A. Constantinople
3. B. St Petersburg
4. A. Baku
5. C. Tehran
6. B. Hong Kong

KATHERINE ROUTLEDGE – AMONG THE STONE GIANTS (p.147)

1. London (British Museum)

2. Washington D.C. (The National Museum of Natural History, also known as The Smithsonian)

3. Paris (The Louvre Museum)

4. Brussels (Art & History Museum)

5. Dunedin (The Otago Museum)

MATTHEW HENSON – UNSUNG HERO OF THE ARCTIC (p.151)

1907: Roald Amundsen
1910: Ernest Shackleton
1927: Charles Lindbergh
1969: Jim Lovell
1970: Neil Armstrong, Edwin 'Buzz' Aldrin, Michael Collins
1995: Jane Goodall
2013: James Cameron

ROBERT FALCON SCOTT – TRAGIC HERO
OF THE ANTARCTIC (p.155)

Name the vessel

EXPLORER	DATE	POSITION	NAME OF LEAD VESSEL
A. James Cook	30th January 1774	71°10'S, 130°W	**Resolution**
B. James Weddell	20th February 1823	74°15'S, 30°12'W	**Jane**
C. James Clark Ross	8th February 1841	78°S, 164°W	**Erebus**
D. James Clark Ross	23rd January 1842	78°10'S, 164°W	**Erebus**
E. Carsten Borchgrevink	16th February 1900	78°50'S, 162°W	**Southern Cross**
F. Robert Falcon Scott	30th December 1902	82°17'S, 165°E	**Discovery**
G. Ernest Shackleton	9th January 1909	88°23'S, 162°E	**Nimrod**
H. Roald Amundsen	14th December 1911	90°	**Fram**

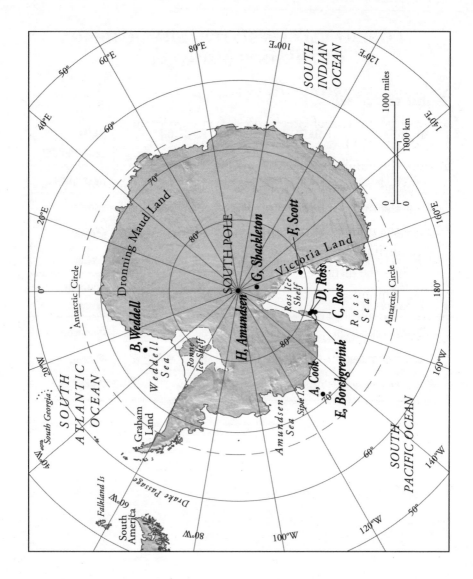

Which creature?

1. B. Killer Whale
2. A. Sea Leopard
3. C. Adélie Penguin
4. B. Blue Whale
5. C. Emperor Penguin
6. B. Snow Petrel

ROALD AMUNDSEN – PIONEERING POLAR EXPLORER (p.161)

Match the numbers to the facts

A. **52** – the number of Greenland sledge dogs Amundsen took in October 1911

B. **56** – the number of minus degrees Celsius that Amundsen had to contend with on his first attempt for the Pole in September 1911

C. **11** – the number of dogs that survived the expedition

D. **99** – the number of days to travel to the Pole and back from Framheim, the team's Antarctic base

E. **1,860** – the distance in nautical miles they had covered

F. **39** – Amundsen's age when he reached the South Pole

G. **34** – the number of days Amundsen beat Scott to the Pole by

H. **19** – total number of crew members on the *Fram*

I. **3,200** – the summit in metres of the Axel Heiberg Glacier

J. **4,500** – the number of calories allocated per person per day

K. **7** – the number of depots Amundsen had constructed along the way

Find the fiction

The lie is: On 3rd August 1958, the USS *Nautilus* completed the first submerged transit of the South Pole. The USS *Nautilus* actually travelled under the North Pole on this date.

Map the route to the explorer

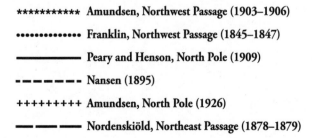

********** Amundsen, Northwest Passage (1903–1906)

•••••••••••••• Franklin, Northwest Passage (1845–1847)

———————— Peary and Henson, North Pole (1909)

– – – – – – Nansen (1895)

+++++++++ Amundsen, North Pole (1926)

— — — Nordenskiöld, Northeast Passage (1878–1879)

ERNEST SHACKLETON – AN EPIC FEAT OF ENDURANCE (p.167)

Message reads:

'Endurance sinking (MORSE CODE)

Last position (CAESAR CIPHER, SHIFTING 3 LETTERS TO THE RIGHT)

69 (BINARY CODE) degrees (BRAILLE), 5 (BINARY CODE) minutes (BRAILLE)

South (MORSE CODE)

51 (BINARY CODE) degrees (BRAILLE), 30 (BINARY CODE) minutes (BRAILLE)

West (MORSE CODE)

Shackleton, October Twenty-Seventh, Nineteen Fifteen' (CAESAR CIPHER, SHIFTING 3 LETTERS TO THE RIGHT)

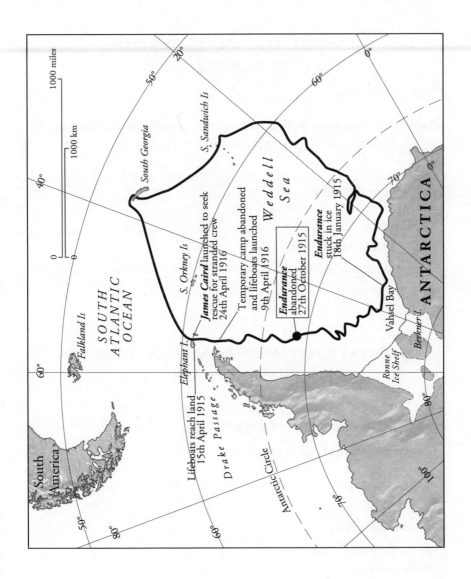

1000 miles

1000 km

0

SOUTH
ATLANTIC
OCEAN

Falkland Is

South
America

South Georgia

S. Sandwich Is

S. Orkney Is

Elephant I.

James Caird launched to seek
rescue for stranded crew
24th April 1916

Temporary camp abandoned
and lifeboats launched
9th April 1916

Endurance
abandoned
27th October 1915

W e d d e l l
S e a

Endurance
stuck in ice
18th January 1915

Lifeboats reach land
15th April 1915

D r a k e   P a s s a g e

Antarctic Circle

ANTARCTICA

Vahsel Bay

*Ronne
Ice Shelf*

Berkner I.

20°
0°

50°

60°

40°

70°

60°

80°

50°

60°

70°

80°

0°

100°

HOWARD CARTER – LEGENDARY EGYPTOLOGIST (p.171)

Find the fiction

Of the 58 people who were present at the opening of Tutankhamun's tomb, only **eight** of them had died within 12 years.

Hieroglyphic code

TO: LORD CARNARVON
FROM: HOWARD CARTER
'At last have made wonderful discovery in Valley; a magnificent tomb with seals intact'

HARRIET CHALMERS ADAMS – A FEARLESS PIONEER (p.175)

Headline: 'Sneaking Past Jaguars'
Society of Women Geographers

1. Amelia Earhart
2. Eleanor Roosevelt
3. Jane Goodall
4. Kathryn Sullivan
5. Sylvia Earle

AMELIA EARHART – INSPIRATIONAL AVIATER (p.179)

1. Pocahontas
2. Frida Kahlo
3. Katharine Hepburn
4. Sylvia Plath
5. Rosa Parks
6. Edith Piaf

BRAINTEASER: Hot chocolate. She also drank a glass of tomato juice and ate a boiled egg during the 18-hour journey.

Record Breaker

1. B. Charles Lindbergh
2. C. Spanish Flu
3. D. Northern Ireland
4. True
5. C. Eleanor Roosevelt
6. A. Librarian

Lost at Sea

FROM	MILES
Oakland, California, USA	325
Burbank, California, USA	450
Tucson, Arizona, USA	1,250
New Orleans, Louisiana, USA	675
Miami, Florida, USA	1,033
San Juan, Puerto Rico	750
Caripito, Venezuela	667
Paramaribo, Suriname (then Dutch Guiana)	1,200
Fortaleza, Brazil	268
Natal, Brazil	1,961
Saint-Louis, Senegal (then French West Africa)	103

FROM	MILES
Dakar, Senegal (then French West Africa)	1,130
Gao, Mali (then French West Africa)	989
Ndjamena, Chad (then French Equatorial Africa)	700
El Fasher, Sudan	501
Khartoum, Sudan	450
Massawa, Ethiopia (then Italian Eritrea)	300
Assab, Ethiopia (then Italian Eritrea)	1,600
Karachi, Pakistan (then India)	1,390
Calcutta, India	335
Sittwe, Myanmar (then Burma)	306
Rangoon, Myanmar (then Burma)	300
Bangkok, Thailand (then Siam)	904
Singapore, Malaysia	560
Bandoeng, Java, Indonesia (then Dutch East Indies)	**355**
Soerabaja, Java, Indonesia (then Dutch East Indies)	**355**
Bandoeng, Java, Indonesia (then Dutch East Indies)	**1,165**
Koepang, Timor, Indonesia	500
Port Darwin, Australia	1,207
Lae, Papau New Guinea (then Territory of New Guinea)	**2,556**
Howland Island	**n/a**

EDMUND HILLARY AND TENZING NORGAY – CONQUERORS OF EVEREST (p.187)

Everest trivia quiz

1. A. 'Forehead in the sky'
2. B. 'Goddess mother of mountains'
3. C. Peak XV
4. C. 80
5. A. 13
6. C. 20,000
7. B. 6
8. C. Kangchenjunga

Spot the untruths

FICTION:

For their achievements, Edmund Hillary, Tenzing Norgay and John Hunt were all knighted by Queen Elizabeth II. (Tenzing Norgay was not knighted; he only ever received the George Medal.)

Norgay broke the record for the deepest dive without swimming aids in 1959, achieving a depth of 100m below sea level off the coast of the Bahamas.

NEIL ARMSTRONG – FIRST MAN ON THE MOON (p.193)

1. A. Sea of Harmony
2. C. Socrates Crater
3. B. 17
4. A. John F. Kennedy Space Center
5. B. Michael Collins
6. B. Montes Pennines
7. False (Ganymede – the largest of Jupiter's moons is the largest planetary satellite in the solar system)
8. True

YURI GAGARIN – THE FIRST PERSON
IN SPACE (p.197)

DATE	CLUE	COUNTRY
12th April 1961	n/a	**Soviet Union**
5th May 1961	n/a	**United States of America**
2nd March 1978	Former name for the country that deposed its government during the Velvet Revolution in 1993	**Czechoslovakia**
27th June 1978	Central European country whose cryptologists performed a vital role in cracking the German Enigma codes during the Second World War	**Poland**
26th August 1978	Former country that was formed from the Soviet Occupation Zone in the wake of the Second World War	**East Germany**
10th April 1979	European country bordering the Black Sea to the east and Romania to the north	**Bulgaria**
26th May 1980	The Danube runs through this country's capital, Budapest	**Hungary**
23rd July 1980	Southeastern country containing the Mekong delta	**Vietnam**
13th September 1980	The most populous country in the Caribbean	**Cuba**
22nd March 1981	Genghis Khan is considered this country's founding father	**Mongolia**
14th May 1981	Contains the historical region of Transylvania	**Romania**
24th June 1982	Country that famously underwent a bloody revolution from 1789 to 1799 that overthrew the monarchy	**France**

DATE	CLUE	COUNTRY
28th November 1983	Former Country who won the FIFA World Cup in 1990 while undergoing reunification	**West Germany**
3rd April 1984	The most populous democracy in the world	**India**
5th October 1984	The world's second largest country by total area	**Canada**
17th June 1985	Country containing both the holy cities of Mecca and Medina	**Saudi Arabia**
30th October 1985	Country with the largest port in Europe	**Netherlands** (Rotterdam is the largest port in Europe)
26th November 1985	Country whose flag features a coat of arms with an eagle sitting on a cactus devouring a serpent	**Mexico**
22nd July 1987	Arab state whose capital was well-known in the Middle Ages for the fine-patterned fabrics produced there	**Syria** (Damascus is the capital)
29th August 1988	Landlocked Asian country that declared independence from Britain in 1919	**Afghanistan**

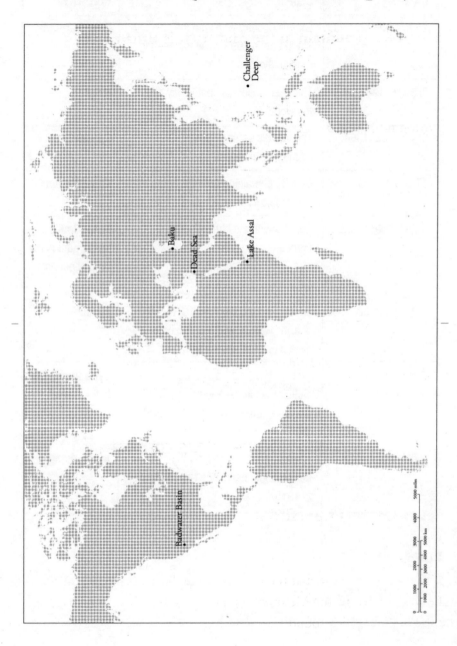

JUNKO TABEI – MOUNTAINEERING LEGEND (p.207)

Match the mountain to the country it is situated in:

Ben Nevis	United Kingdom
Mount Logan	Canada
Mount Olympus	Greece
Mount Kenya	Kenya
Kilimanjaro	Tanzania
Mount Ararat	Turkey
Elbrus	Russia
Aoraki (Mount Cook)	New Zealand
Puncak Jaya	Indonesia
Mount Kosciuszko	Australia
Grossglockner	Austria
Pico da Neblina	Brazil
Pico Bolívar	Venezuela
Denali (Mount McKinley)	United States of America
Pico de Orizaba (Citlaltépetl)	Mexico

RANULPH FIENNES – 'THE GREATEST LIVING EXPLORER' (p.219)

Separating fact from fiction

FICTION:

On his way to an event at the Royal Geographical Society in 2003, he was arrested by the Metropolitan Police for carrying an ice pick on the London Underground.

In 1981, while trekking across Queen Elizabeth Land in Antarctica, he wrestled a young female polar bear who had entered his tent.

Fiennes in Figures

65 – Age when he reached the summit of Everest

97 – The number of days it took Sir Ranulph Fiennes to walk across Antarctica

94 – The position Sir Ranulph Fiennes appeared on the *Daily Telegraph*'s list of Top 100 Living Geniuses

130 – The number of beats per minute his cardiac surgeon warned him not to exceed during his seven marathons in seven days challenge

13 – The number of times doctors attempted to restart his heart after a heart attack in 2003

156 – The number of miles he ran in the Marathon des Sables – an annual ultra-marathon in the Sahara Desert – in 2015

24 – The number of books Sir Ranulph Fiennes has written

10 – The number of UK universities to present him with an honorary doctorate or fellowship

3 – The number of attempts it took Sir Ranulph Fiennes to scale Everest

ELLEN MACARTHUR – RECORD-BREAKING SAILOR (p.217)

1. A. Muesli bars/porridge
2. B. Albatross
3. B. An arthritic robot
4. C. Champagne/Neptune
5. A. Burning hot wire/Yes
6. B. The White Cliffs of Dover
7. A. Richard Branson

FELICITY ASTON – RECORD-BREAKING
POLAR EXPLORER (p.221)

1. Robert Falcon Scott
2. Vivian Fuchs
3. Ranulph Fiennes
4. Edmund Hillary
5. Ernest Shackleton
6. Ginny Fiennes
7. Jane Francis
8. Private Frazer

Walking the Nile

Rwanda
Tanzania
Uganda
South Sudan
Sudan
Egypt

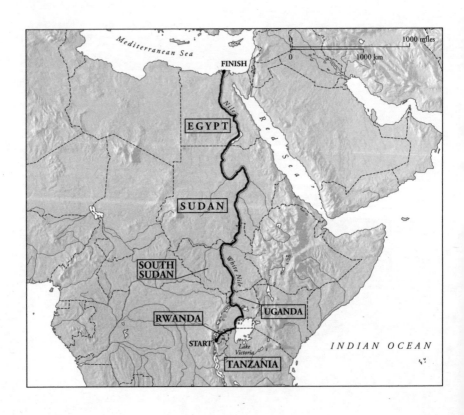

Walking the Americas

Mexico
Belize
Guatemala
Honduras
Nicaragua
Costa Rica
Panama
Colombia

THE ROYAL GEOGRAPHICAL SOCIETY
FAMILY QUIZ

Answers

1.
(i) D: Robert Falcon Scott, 1911
(ii) B: Ernest Shackleton, 1915
(iii) A: Douglas Mawson, 1912
(iv) C: Roald Amundsen, 1912

2 C: Australia

3.
A: Pennsylvania (as in Pennsylvania [Penn] Station)
B: Georgia (held in Augusta, Georgia)
C: New Hampshire
D: North Carolina

4 A: London, England

5 B: Vasco da Gama

6. Jacques Cousteau

7 C: Edwin

8. 3 (Saint Kitts and Nevis; Saint Lucia; and Saint Vincent and the Grenadines)

9.
A: Paris (where there are numerous replicas)
B: Bordeaux
C: Las Vegas
D: Rio de Janeiro

10. La Sagrada Família, Barcelona

11. Copenhagen, Denmark

12 C: The Louvre, Paris

13 A: The Eiffel Tower, Paris

14. The San Andreas Fault

15. Honshu, Hokkaido, Kyushu, Shikoku

16. Romania, Russia, Rwanda

17 C: Chile

18.
A: Channel Tunnel
B: Empire State Building
C: Itaipu Dam
D: Panama Canal

19 A: 73mph

20 B: Jurassic Coast

21.
(i) The Eternal City	C: Rome
(ii) The Fair City	D: Dublin
(iii) The Lion City	E: Singapore
(iv) The Forbidden City	F: Beijing
(v) The Pearl of the Adriatic	A: Dubrovnik
(vi) The Big Easy	B: New Orleans

22 A: Canada and the USA

23 C: The Caspian Sea

24.
AUSTRIA
BULGARIA
CROATIA
GERMANY
HUNGARY
MOLDOVA
ROMANIA
SERBIA
SLOVAKIA
UKRAINE

25.
ARKANSAS
ILLINOIS
IOWA
KENTUCKY
LOUISIANA
MISSISSIPPI
MINNESOTA
MISSOURI
TENNESSEE
WISCONSIN

26 C: La Paz, Bolivia

27 A: Amsterdan, which is situated approximately 2 metres below sea level

28 B: Yellowstone

29 B: Brazil (27 stars). The flag of Uzbekistan has 12 stars and Honduras has 5.

30 C: Monaco and Indonesia

31 B: Francisco Pizarro

32. They have all replaced former capitals of their respective countries.

33 C: Atacama Desert

34 A: The Zambezi

35 A: Alaska

36. Melbourne, Australia

37. London

38.
Belgrade
Belmopan
Brasilia
Brussels
Budapest

39.
I = Islamabad (Pakistan)
Q = Quito (Ecuador)
U = Ulaanbaatar (Mongolia)
Z = Zagreb (Croatia)

40.–50.

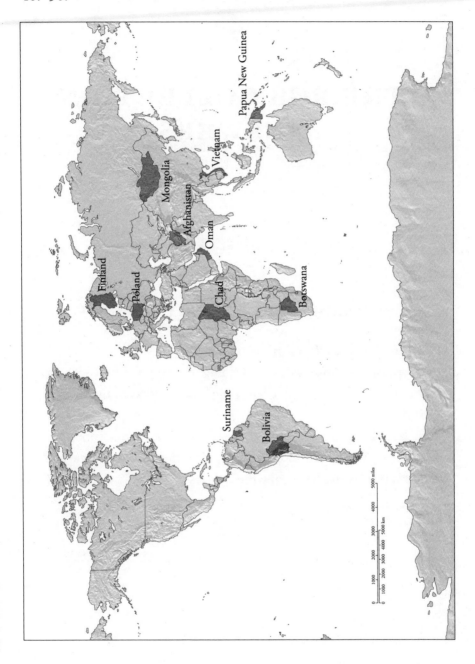

THE RGS COLLECTION ANSWERS

QUIZ 1

PTOLEMY – PIONEERING POLYMATH

London appears as '**Londiniu**(m)'

Bath appears as '**Aque calide**', meaning 'hot water', but it was also known as 'Aquae Sulis', after Sulis, the local goddess of the thermal springs

Winchester appears as '**Venta** (Belgarum)', with 'Venta' coming from the Common Brittonic 'Uentā', meaning 'town or place' and 'Belgarum' after the local tribe the Belgae

IBN BATTUTA – THE GREATEST TRAVELLER
WHO LIVED?

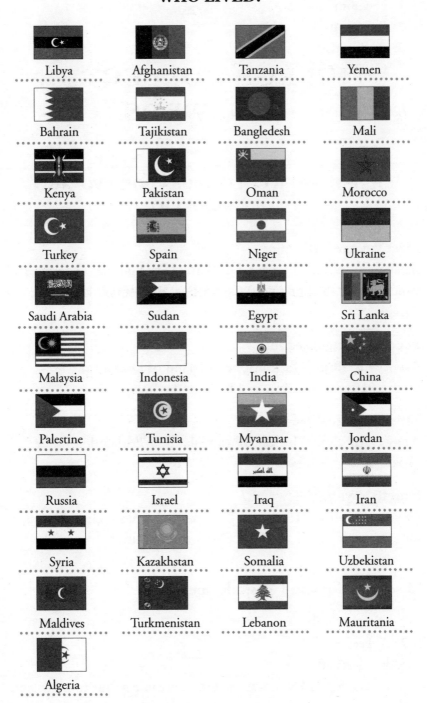

Libya

Afghanistan

Tanzania

Yemen

Bahrain

Tajikistan

Bangledesh

Mali

Kenya

Pakistan

Oman

Morocco

Turkey

Spain

Niger

Ukraine

Saudi Arabia

Sudan

Egypt

Sri Lanka

Malaysia

Indonesia

India

China

Palestine

Tunisia

Myanmar

Jordan

Russia

Israel

Iraq

Iran

Syria

Kazakhstan

Somalia

Uzbekistan

Maldives

Turkmenistan

Lebanon

Mauritania

Algeria

Ancient cities – missing answers

1. C. Cairo
2. B. Medina
3. A. Baghdad
4. C. Alexandria
5. B. Constantinople
6. C. Delhi

CHRISTOPHER COLUMBUS – FOUR VOYAGES OF DISCOVERY

First Voyage – Blue line
Answer to clue: The Island of Santa [St] Maria in the Azores, which shares its name with Columbus' flagship on his first voyage.

Second Voyage Red line
Answer to clue: The Caribbean Island of Dominica (named after the Latin word for 'Sunday').

Third Voyage Green line
Answer to clue: The Caribbean island of Trinidad (Spanish for 'Trinity').

Fourth Voyage Yellow line
Answer to clue: He named the island Gracias a Dios (Spanish for 'Thanks to God'), off the Coast of Honduras.

Miscalculations and Misjudgements

1. C. 4,500 miles
2. A. Pear
3. B. Mermaid
4. B. The *Santa Maria* was carried by ocean currents towards land,

running aground on a sandbank and sinking the following afternoon.

QUIZ 2

Mungo Park

Map Locations

1. Pisania
2. Medina
3. Kemmoo
4. Jarra
5. Sego
6. Silla

Anagrams

1. Indigo
2. Antelope/Ostrich
3. Alligators/Hippopotamus
4. Crocodile
5. Gunpowder
6. Guinea Fowl/Partridge
7. Mangrove

CHARLES DARWIN – REVOLUTIONARY
NATURALIST

1. Cholera
2. Mauritius
3. An earthquake
4. *Paradise Lost* by John Milton
5. St Elmo's fire
6. The abolition of slavery
7. Vampire bats

Guess the Animal

1. B. Duck-billed Platypus
2. A. Giant Tortoise
3. B. Marine Iguana
4. B. Frog

QUIZ 3

JOHN C FRÉMONT – THE PATHFINDER

1. San Francisco
2. Los Angeles
3. San Diego
4. Santa Fe
5. Vancouver
6. Sacramento
7. Omaha

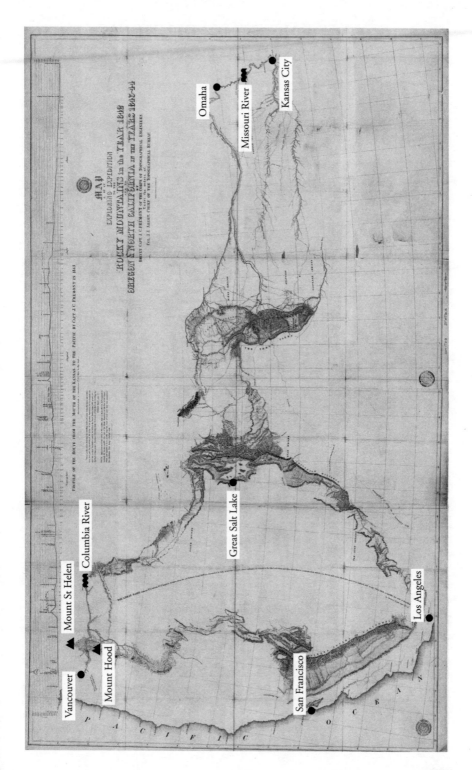

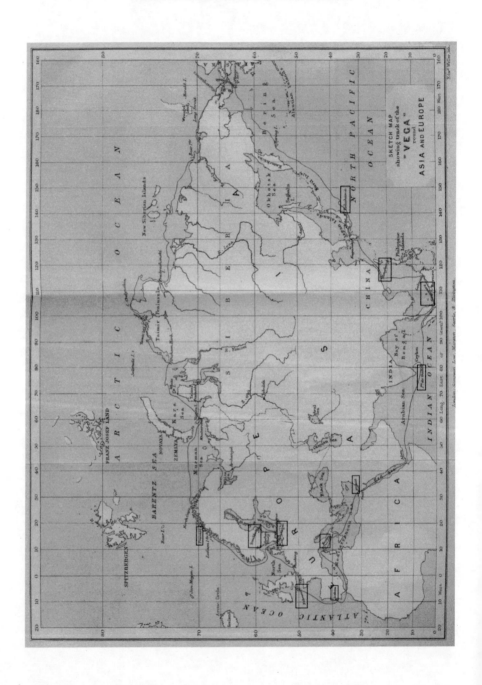

Arctic creatures

1. Arctic Fox
2. Polar Bear
3. Snowy Owl
4. Reindeer
5. Narwhal
6. Mammoth
7. Aurora Borealis (Northern Lights)

FREYA STARK

(From left to right, top to bottom)
Turkey, Yemen, Syria, Egypt, Kuwait, Iran, Lebanon, Saudi Arabia, Palestine, Iraq, Israel, Jordan.

ACKNOWLEDGEMENTS

It's been an absolute pleasure working through our Collections and compiling our first ever puzzle book! A big thank you to all the staff at the Society and a special thanks to Alasdair MacLeod, Julie Cole and Professor Joe Smith for all their time and effort in bringing this book to life. Thanks, too, to Joel Simons for coming to us with the idea, and to Madiya Altaf, Sophia Walker, Jess Tackie, Emily Rough and Naomi Green and all the team at Bonnier Books UK, as well as Graeme Andrew for his masterful typesetting and to Mike Adams for the additional cartography.

Nathan Joyce: I'd like to thank my wife Tarah for putting up with me typing away loudly in the attic for weeks on end (something I'm still doing as I write this). I'd also like to mention my Geography-teaching brother Dan Brown. Several of the questions are very specifically designed to make you tear your hair out on Christmas Day while trying to work out the answers. And finally to the RGS, for allowing me access to their extraordinary Collections. I felt a bit like Harry Potter entering Hogwarts when I was invited there.

MAPS

Front cover: 'Polus Artieus', from 'Atlas sive cosmographicae meditationes de fabrica mundi et fabricati figura', 1595.

Collections Quiz 1: A section from 'Map of the world' from a Ptolemaic atlas published by J. Reger (Ulm, 1486).

Collections Quiz 2: A section from 'Map of the globe centred on the north pole and superimposed on the south pole', from 'Cartes et Tables de la Géographie Physique ou Naturelle' by Philippe Buache, published Paris, c.1780.

Collections Quiz 3: A section from World Map (Nova Orbis Tabula) from 'Nicolass Visscher Atlas Minor', c. 1719.

The Puzzles (p. 1): A section from 'A map of the world in which is represented the moral state of all mankind particularly the progress Christianity is making through the World'. Designed and drawn by James Sabine, 1815 and engraved by Michael Thomson, World, 1815.

RGS Family quiz (p. 228): Map showing Shackleton's 'Furthest South' during his 1907-1909 British Antarctic ('Nimrod') Expedition.

**Royal
Geographical
Society**
Enterprises

Commercial activities
supporting the charity

JOIN THE ROYAL GEOGRAPHICAL SOCIETY (WITH IBG)

The Royal Geographical Society (with IBG) is the UK's learned society and professional body for geography, as well as being a membership organisation and a charity.

The Society is the perfect home for those who are curious about the world's people, places and environments, and how they interact. Membership is open to all – with different categories to suit all types of interests and involvement. Benefits include access to a huge range of resources including our historical Collections, topical events across the country, and the opportunity to connect with others who share their curiosity.

We have a range of membership options available to suit everyone with an interest in geography including Young Geographer, Fellowship and Ordinary Membership.

For more information on how you could benefit from being a member of the Royal Geographical Society (with IBG), see www.rgs.org/joinus

FINAL NOTE

We hope you enjoyed *The Royal Geographical Society Puzzle Book*. We certainly enjoyed putting it together! During the process every endeavour was made to make sure the book is free from error. However, should you spot any incorrect information please do not hesitate to contact hello@blinkpublishing.co.uk.